The Day I Wasn't There

AGM COLLECTION

AVANT-GARDE & MODERNISM

The Day I Wasn't There

HÉLÈNE CIXOUS

Translated from the French by Beverley Bie Brahic

Northwestern

University Press

Evanston

Illinois

Northwestern University Press
www.nupress.northwestern.edu

Printed in the United States of America

10 9 8 7 6 5 4 3 2 1

ISBN 0-8101-2364-9

Library of Congress Cataloging-in-Publication data are available
from the Library of Congress.

Contents

The Day I Wasn't There

How to get rid of the memory of a fault which looms up out of the distant past? It is dawn, it is back again, I absolutely have to bury it. I shut it up in a clay pot. Then I dug very deep into the hardened cold ground. Without of course telling anyone what was in the pot. Then I shoved it—a pot about as big as a little quart kettle—into the ground—and I covered it up again for a long time with earth, with ice, in spite of the presence of passersby and children who had no idea what I was ridding myself of in this little improvised coffin.

I washed my hands, wiped off my cheeks some tears that had got away from me.

My crimes, I thought, were all committed in Algeria. This one here is a fault, and it is not mine.

You are warding off the dim nestling the nestled dimling, I told myself, and I opened my eyes.

All night, I'd kept it at bay, without driving it away, though, because driving a presence away by getting up or hissing at it, it's what not to do, one must doze on, despite the vague rustling over there in the corner by the window, perhaps it's the cat, perhaps the presence, it's wiser not to notice, to insist on serenity until the thing melts away.

He was always gentle and conciliatory, I thought, and I saw myself thinking in furtive thoughts, using the third person, in order not to give the minute visitor a chance to become familiar. But this defense system, I didn't mean to put it up. It rises all by itself like a thick but translucent fog between my body and the invaders. I didn't even let his name flutter on my lips. But the name floated at half-mast in my mind, the emblem of a bitter-toothed fatality, like the handkerchief soiled with mourning that a mother waves on the train platform. The train shudders off, the child leaves. Without knowing, you know it is forever.

Did I know when I turned away, denying everything, denying the necessity, denying the event, denying the prediction, denying the error and the truth, denying the cruelty, denying the innocence, denying the patient, the hopeful words, denying each and every fault, denying the facts, the features, the eyes, the mouth the tongue the hands the nose, did I know I was denying who I was denying, did I know I kept him in me out of me, from then on in the out of me which makes, in the mined hollow of my nights, a nest where my little nestling forever broods?

With *him,* I thought, all the words of being, of having, of being able, of going, all of them wavered and collapsed. That's why it was always hard for me to talk about it, the fault of language.

Feather-headed fossil of an unfledged child, that's *what it is;* but still it shifts around there and it rustles softly without violence the way a specter gropes for the latch that's been changed in the meantime, rubbing itself against the door, never suspecting it's been denied.

Where was I at station time? Between my room and my mother's house stretched plains, plateaus, coast ranges, seas, nowhere do I see the threshold of his disappearance. She must have put him in a basket. She must have covered him with a sheet, it's all you need in this heat. She must have taken the plane with the little born-peacemaker. Later on he turns up again in the rooms of the Clinic, that's where I bend again over his cradle come from afar, I recall the bright-colored triple rattle shaken in his face, I was playing with the rattle I remember, I scrutinized the distant face, from the earth I wasn't able to see the expression on the face of the moon, this didn't mean it didn't have one. Eyes scrunched up, I tried in vain yet I tried, with my feeble vision, to bring him to the light.

It is the First of May 1999, my son the living has breezed in to pick up the family papers. On the threshold the wind my son suggests going to the movies where I never go. He goes out. It is the first time in my entire life that the family papers have left the house. My breasts are sore. Messages. It's the sons, I think. The sons at fever pitch. I listen to the radio. Dawn and the enumeration of the Daily Crimes. The rest doesn't interest me. The last few months, if I open a book, if I tear at an envelope, I am chosen by the demons. I could escape from them, but I don't. I enter the cages, I tread on their excrement. Ecstasy.

I look for an explanation.

In the mail an envelope says: Open up! Photo! Romania! I open. On the photo a little girl staring straight out. She holds up an arm and on the other side a rosy little apricot. I look closer. It's a stump, a withered fruit. The letter tells all. The ordinary little girl smiles, trustful, a real one, the stump is sweet. The letter explains. Little Irina aged two was gobbled up one night past the elbow by another Irina, aged twelve, dying of hunger who ate her fill. Beginning with the fingers? With the forearm. The little one cried? She screamed with pain in the orphaned orphanage but the one exhausted caretaker for ninety-six children in a single room didn't want to get up. Sleep! Sleep! I want to sleep, she cried in her sleep. That's all? The letter doesn't know what to say. Poor Irina, poor Irina. Such innocence! Such innocence! Later, one hasn't the heart for innocence, they let themselves die of hunger. What cruelty: the words: *innocence: cruelty.* Hunger pounces on them and devours them in a single gulp. Or maybe Irina stopped devouring when she was still hungry but less hungry nonetheless? What a lot of questions! Who will answer for Irina and for Irina? Are they still of this world, I wondered. But what does it mean, world? There was never any world, there was never any world world.

It is hunger that devoured the forearm and the hand. I say *devoured* and not *ate* for during the meal Irina was not eating, she was rushing, not thinking about it. Now Irina and Irina are still alive if diminished and augmented. No harm done, just a tragedy. It's all the other fault.

What was the name of the caretaker in this story? "Irina" I pronounce softly the soft name which doesn't know what it says in the void and the absence. Peace, now! Then I wrote a check, for having looked at the photo. Hadn't I been into the circus tent? When you look at a monstrous child led by two men and a nurse who claim to be the uncle the aunt and the doctor in order to make a few pennies showing it because of its estrangedness, you have to get your change purse out. Each time wondering how much — how much is it worth, this inestimable pain. It's all calculated: That's how it is: You pay, and you toss the photo in the bin, or vice versa. The price of peace: Pay, now. Millions of photos of stumps in the bin. Discarding it, I'm only discarding my miserable glance at it. But it's too late. I obeyed the order of the envelope: Open up! Come in! See!

So my mother said:—I think the money we send over there, we don't know whose pocket it ends up in. It's absolutely atrocious, one can't even imagine such a thing. And none of the other children woke up? One shouldn't believe everything they say. It's just advertising. All children are not monsters. All the same, anything is possible.

I'm going to buy some mussels for tonight, they're very fresh at the farm.

I could tell that she was thinking about the shells in which God molds the infinite forms of his great work including my mother, myself, the Irinas, and everything we call against nature (but which for Him is nothing out of the ordinary).

The telephone has just rung. Nobody there. When there's nobody on the line I know it's God thinking. Loud and clear. I say: yes, yes, to the phone and I hang up, without cutting Him off. Oh I tell myself that it is perhaps not God but on the contrary, it is perhaps a wrong number, but I don't believe it. I only believe that it's God, therefore it is.

Everything in this world and in the others depends on how we read it.

My Three-Legged Dog

Archives of 1 May 1999

It was the first blue day of the year.

Blue as an angel I said. It slipped out. But my mother wasn't listening.

We set off very early for the Bois. I always want to arrive before everybody else.—Where?—Where. Where it begins. Just before the sound and the fury, perhaps. It happens every year: I go to the Bois to add to my book of never-to-be-forgotten days.—Never forget what?—Never to forget: Come back to oneself. It's a matter of taking the same walks, every year there's the miraculous non-miracle of re-beginning and re-budding. It's the law. And yet: I can't get over it. We take note that we are still here. No forgetting along the walks. Then there was a rip in the murmured silence. The traumas began. The rape of the lake: plastic bags simulations of lumpy carcasses, banged-up *cans*. Two gray geese screamed alarm like sirens on the bank: It was a swan cruising, stiff-necked: No geese allowed! No geese allowed! The two geese didn't dare and screamed haunted by forebodings of massacre. Water off bounds! patrolled the brandished swan. I went down toward the bank armed with the pussy willows of before all memory, armed with the too-light catkins of chestnuts that I pitched violently, fistfuls of them, at the swan crying angrily mean, cruel swan, cruel mean! Go away! Go away! Note that I didn't insult it, the enemy being a swan, I didn't shout bastard! or brute! or dirty rat. I cried swan, I summoned it go away go away. Slowly the swan veered off obedient. Immediately the two geese set sail.

I thought about meanness. I thought about powerlessness. I thought about the will to power and about the powerlessness of the will and about the force of power. I thought about the mainspring of the soul: how to think the unthinkable while it is happening.

And to which god were the two geese screeching their prayers and their imprecations?

About the drake which yesterday was trying to drown its duck and there was nothing I could do or at least I did nothing. He mounts it he grips the little beige head in his beak and he holds it under the water to annihilate it. I screamed. Yesterday too. Deaf as a post. I could scream till I was blue in the face. The power of assassination was absolute. My cries were drying in the air. I did not wade completely dressed into the polluted pond. I am telling the truth. I went away, disgusted. I thought no more about the drake with his duck. But the inaudible cries of the duck under the water of the back of my mind added themselves to everything else that would keep us from living if we thought about it.

We were on the island nestled in the middle of the lake. What is a lake isle? For a while any persecuted person can find shelter there, it's the cradle, and it's the trap. Once the period of respite has passed you are caught and besieged. We were embarked on the island and it was the sweet luxury of metaphor, ship house shelter ark desert that's when: when my temporary deafness ceased. For a quarter of an hour I had not been letting myself hear the distant cry, my hearing busy with the buzzing of young, hardly formed flies. It was a yelping which, once heard, became inextinguishable, inevitable. The creature was insisting, superhumanly. We were all under a dreadful spell: my mother, my daughter, me, a stout little lady, and two pooches humanized with ribbons and barrettes, all six of us bound in a single spell by the distant barking.—Who is it? I say.—For half an hour. Says the lady held for half an hour in the note of uninterrupted hope. As long as the cry lasts we are unable to move. It was a young voice and it was crying crying crying don't breathe cry not breathing cry crying. You really can't go away. The voice is speaking *to you.*

At last I saw it. I glimpsed it, not very well. Because of the freshness, the youth, I asked who is that crying, what creature, with what angel's voice?— It's a Tintin dog, said the lady with the beribbonned daughters. And she had that look: struggling not to let it become the awful pity. At that moment finally I set eyes on the dog, and I will never be able to act as if I hadn't seen it. In the middle of the spring meadow with its tender cloak, on the other side of the lake, cries cries cries a neatly drawn white fox terrier with a black spot on its left side, it was calling like a spirit that has never known discouragement. It was so long, I began to have doubts. At the end it bounced, it spurted from the fabric of the meadow and I saw that it was jumping on three legs, it has three legs I say, it only has three legs my daughter says, it's missing a leg says the lady, it is missing its right hind leg says my mother, this leg suddenly we were all missing it, or rather it hit us, it was running fast, running with all its strength right and left meanwhile a lady arrived on a bike. She stopped and gave us the explanation, saying: It doesn't belong to anybody, and there's nobody. And she said: They abandoned it, it's the First of May. It was the First of May the day they abandon the little dog, three legs is all it takes, one does not kill, on abandoning day it is always very blue, the meadow is a human allusion, there is no one on earth, the moment they let it go in the meadow the dog gives a little drunken leap, the grass is so fragrant that doesn't keep him from feeling ashamed because he smells all the perfumes of all the thoughts, and although he is not guilty there is a fault, the fault of a leg, the fault of time, the fault of patience, the fault of tolerance, all these faults are not his fault but he is accountable nonetheless, because of his fault of a leg, you need one to bear the weight of the family sins, so it's him, it's him who has failed to be pardoned.

The bike lady was saying: No caretaker the First of May. The day of abandonment and no witness. The dog lady said: Sooner or later he'll find a restaurant. And off they went.

Left to chance again, the stray frisked about calling: Nice! nice! nice! I am nice! Besides with three legs you are still good for running jumping eating playing, it's only slightly fewer legs, it doesn't keep you from existing, I am nice! nice! nice!

Me I say nothing.—Every year they abandon the First of May the bike lady said.

The First of May, feast of the abandon. Instead of killing. The dog acquitted. Pardon! Pardon! Pardon. Pardoned.

And me too? And me too. And you too.

What to do

I abandoned

I have been abandoned

And that's what has always abandoned us,

—The Answer—

Already when I was three and so many abandons and things abandoned, myself included,

I didn't know, already I did not know what to do with such and so many abandons

Already I felt so forsaken on the one hand and so forsaking on the other

and all eaten up with knowing how to ask already at the age of three and not-ever-knowing what how to answer, with all the forsaken of the earth what to do,

with all these dogs in whose image we have been created in order to be forsaken, punished for having lost a leg which however doesn't prevent anyone from running and crying very loud and pleading saying "I-still-am."

Already when I was three, in Oran,

what should could would I have been done seen

when I was already an atheist on the earth

crying for a quarter of an hour without stopping

the cry why have you forsaken me.

Already I had the look of a three-legged fox terrier

The worst is not to have less it is this less that doesn't keep you from existing in order to be abandoned on the First of May

each year all those who are driven into the meadow

having only three of four legs is this a crime

round and round, rounding up your thoughts

—should I go and get the dog—

my heart swung back—forth—back

—back—for one whole minute—

My mother at my side was thinking: If you go get that dog, I'm going to slam the door, I'm going to go away.

At her side I thought: Ah! if only you hadn't been with me! Then anguish. Sadly anguished: Would I have adopted it? the question in me asked itself—and I didn't know how to say loud and clear: yes.

Because at that moment the cat in me thought: If you bring an animal back to the house the way you did to me last year, coming through the door with another creature in your arms that I thought belonged to me, I will burst into terrible cat sobs and I will rake every face with my claws until I die.

My daughter beside me thought: I am going to break into a heart-rending cry I shall burst, I am bursting. Let's go, let's go, I am bloodied.

In conclusion—

In conclusion I thought: Dear dog cherished on three legs, everything keeps us apart including myself.

He with his terrible doggy freedom which was pleading: Take me, pleaded and pleading believed. Believed.

My mother tugged on my leash. I followed. The dog followed me with his eyes, I had his eyes in the back of my neck. Head down I walked off along the path with my mother.

—A three-legged dog needs to be ssssshot, and that's all, said my mother, adding four *s*'s to the word *shot,* and shooting it at me with all the strength of her conviction. For, to strike, she never uses a knife or a blunt or sharp instrument: Her operative mode is to increase the number of consonants.

She sslipped her arm into mine

and I let the stray race back and forth in the meadow. Far away. Far away, its dwindling voice. Kinship increased. Its voice crossed the world. Will someone else respond to it?

One more dog I didn't save. I strolled amongst the roses, my heart bleeding, petals clenched. Once upon a time my cat was saved and in being saved saved me and since then I have not saved any other creature nor other creatures or perhaps I have but not on purpose since I have not been saved, but everything kept me from it, I'm not going to accuse anyone, my cat doesn't want to share me and I don't do battle with it, I have already chased two cats away for love of my cat in weakness and in strength, perforce, forced, but I am not going to accuse anyone, no one wants to share and me too neither I don't want to divide myself into hostile cats and I don't do battle with myself.

I would like to find the argument that pardons.

I am a woman who always has courthouses in her head, all because I was not deported, that can neither be regretted nor not regretted nor be said, it can only try to blunt the thorns on the roses, a never-ending trial, my mother neither was not deported, and she never deports herself from the straight and narrow, without regret and without regret for regret. Whereas I, separated from deportation by a verdant meadow and a deep blue sea, I have always in my skull a bench of judges who abandon me to a searing absence of punishment.

Later in the morning, with all these animals in my head, some female, the others threatening, the trusting, and the birds which I always think my cat is thinking of, I forgot the fox terrier.

When I got home I told my cat all about it. She curled up in the May light in my image, offering her white belly to my lips which she does not have to fear sharing. I smiled at her, there is nothing she likes as much as my smile, I smiled at her with a little abandon stuck in my guts. Stretched out on the bed, I leafed through the big book of archive photos from Algeria. All the photos, Jews, Arabs, brave settlers, leading citizens, the Kabyle woman, the rich European and his wife, from 1882 to 1945 and nobody smiling agas, horsemen, kaids, the black servant, the dignified old man, players in a game of chess, douar chief, candy seller, ouled naïl, free-woman-capable-of-inspiring-Delacroix, French family settled in Miliana, colonists about to make their fortune, travelers on the Setif–Constantine bus line and nobody from 1882 to 1945 to smile.

I lived in this country. I knew.

Already when I was three years old, Boulevard Seguin, in Oran, I saw the photos this country would leave. I ran up the steaming streets as fast as I could so my cut leg wouldn't trip me up. But I could never get past the square with the cathedral without being stopped, petrified by the enormity of that face hardened into the gold.

All the time I lived in Algeria my native land not stopping going to primary school then to secondary school as if in exile, I was dreaming of arriving one day in Algeria though it was my own native land, to find the door at last while I was going every day to school along a corridor of to my eyes irascible streets, and yet so fragrant, skirting the invisible walls reserved for immigrants who keep step with them whenever they go from one part of town to another, I was dreaming of one day entering my native land as I used to wade into the welcoming sea, to melt in, to be part of it, no longer prowl around the outside of the body of my city in the heart of town, which is what was happening to me daily, even on the post office square, even on the government square, even on the city hall square, even on the cathedral square, I wanted so badly to be one day invited to a wedding or a birth, and then go, my heart pounding, finally penetrate to the heart of my kind and be born of them like a human being or another, like all the other human beings save us, I saw myself at last with henna on the palms of my hands and feet, I saw myself at last stuffing my mouth with couscous with beans and whey, my hands full of the sugary grain, the difference with the couscous at my grandmother's being the henna and the hands, but I never found anything but closed doors in my way, I see myself knocking at an olive green door or an almond green door banging my little fists on them and squealing: Come in! or Come in! for a long time for nothing in my ignorance of the password, if there was one. Another difference or another misunderstanding it's that I was smiling. On all the photos I can see myself smile, I was always smiling, there was nothing I could do about it, though the others were not smiling and perhaps I offended their no-smiling and without any reason, no inhabitant of the Two Worlds having any reason to smile without mistrust while I was living in Algeria. With my mouth open and all my teeth gleaming on display I was like a wound that I kept reopening even when I wanted so badly for the scar to heal. My smilingness was beyond my control, I was ajar, I signified come in, I was miming what I wanted and not really what I had to offer, I was longing for visits, I was expecting travelers, I had the soul of an innkeeper set up in the desert, come, come, I said and my eyes followed with devotion the pointy swallows cutting out the high blue metal with their scissors. Nobody came. We were too widowed a family, too woman, too girlish, we were bad, we were repulsive and not veiled. And me trusting, in the stubborn expectancy of no one. Without fear but not without anguish every morning, schoolbag in hand, off I went again to try and gain admittance to the heart of hearts of this native city Oran followed by Algiers which in no time at all slipped out of sight in a flutter of mists and veils, I was running blinded guided by my sense of smell between columns of spicy perfumes, while ahead of me, to my immense dismay, vanished, snatched away by some incomprehensible sleight of hand, now the cathedral leaving only the proof of the equestrian statue already half-swallowed up, now the Municipal Theater, now the harbor entry and drowned quays where gigantic barrels of wine were bobbing, each time everything had been but was curtly denied me, and these denials felt like fatal betrayals, it wasn't fair, I couldn't get used to it, this whole city which I loved nonetheless was leagued against me in an attempt to throw me off balance by means of my vision, a powerful argument for someone as nearsighted as I for these brutal mists, these vanishing museums and churches, these sudden doglegs in the avenues, perhaps they were my fault, my misdoing, perhaps it was I who missaw what was right under my nose all along. So I was always ready to accuse myself of the wrongs that I suffered.

One evening when I am coming out of the Theater after dancing class suddenly I am struck with limping. This time the spell takes me by the feet, I advance as if I were walking backward, my sandals attack me, I have two dogs at my ankles, one crushes my toes, the other wags at heel, I stumble and trip, obstructed, trapped, it's already dark when I finally manage to get cast up at the house, I drop at last I have the right to drop since I no longer have to hold my head up in public, I collapse, crumple up on my knees head dangling. Then I notice two strange shoes on my feet, one brown and the other gray that I'd never seen before, causes of my misery and consequences of my unreflecting shortsightedness and my credulity. For I always head straight for the supernatural in Algeria. Meanwhile my own sandals abandoned in the changing room where nobody will have wanted to inflict them on themselves. You get the wrong shoes and it's exile wandering and solitude. You walk with your feet twisted up, mocking, foreign, and all time is out of joint, shelter recedes infinitely, the road climbs sheer as a wall in front of this uninhabitable, footloose body. And all the magic of my city out of sight. A city that I knew by foot in every sense. Losing time, losing blood, but not the earth.

Still the First of May

But later, I take the metro under the earth to go to the Cinema. I was going to see a film that I do not want to see but it's a duty I know. *Un Spécialiste.* Repellent name. But impelled by my son the wind and drawn by the word that repels me, pulled this way and that off I go taking the way through the dark. As soon as there is *species, special,* I grow tense. Going to see *the specialist* was like delivering my myopia to the Cyclops to size up. More precisely handing my two quivering eyes like two fuzzy-eyed lambs over to be judged. In order to see the film called *A Specialist* it is necessary to have in your soul a region which is carefully insulated from the rest of your being so that the evil cannot ooze out indefinitely. To say I wanted to see it calls for an explanation: It is precisely the film one *especially-does-not-want* to see one wants nonetheless to see, just for that reason, because there is refusal repugnance and danger, that's how one day I ended up reading a book I *especially-did-not-want* to read because the minute I opened it I saw that everything took place in one sanatorium or another, places I force myself not to write *satanorium* by mistake, because for one reason or another if there is one place in the world I dread more than a prison or camp, because of the evil sorts of metamorphosis that happen to us there, it's the place called by the Latin word *sanatorium:* And likewise I have a repugnance for the Latin word in French *spécialiste,* and likewise for the same Latin word in German. And in the same way after a losing battle with myself I end up writing a book that I *especially-did-not-want* to write.

Destiny is when we end up doing what we *especially-did-not-want* to do. And that's a thing I can't explain.

For a long time I did not want to go to see *Un Spécialiste* until the day when convinced by my son and overcoming myself I went, because it being the First of May Labor Day, it's what I had to do that day. There was nothing else to do. Except give in and go to this tale. That day, a day of rest, encircled day, day apart, enclaved day, day to remember and day to abandon, day dedicated to work and its opposite, opposite day, day of war and carnival is the day I went, as to the sanatorium my father, to make myself sick. I owed myself the minutes of the Eichmann trial. It was my job for the day. Plus it was Saturday. There was only the law and no prohibition, or rather all the prohibition pulsating in the law: Thou shalt go. So I complied. I went. On my way I bought no lily of the valley neither on the right nor on the left I noted it well. I went straight to the sana and no loitering— it was not the day of woods and meadows for me. My job was to go where I knew I'd be waiting for me. To the interrogatory.

In the course of the day I descended into the earth again and again, I climbed back up from under the earth, I walked on the earth, I crossed bridges for hours, I went along roads without names it was spring I saw a poppy lit up all by itself on the tip of its stalk I descended into the earth again and again, my dead caught me by surprise there, one in particular, one of my sons, of whom I never thought anymore, and who came back to me on that day from a to z, I wept, because there was no one, no one to weep for my dog, no one to remember him, I never think of him anymore, I crossed the underside of the city several times in opposite directions, I saw the linings of things everywhere there was shadow of crime and shadow of abandon and entwined roots of good and of evil.

I am porous. For nothing, for a brief encounter, for brushing up against a phrase tinted with this or that accent that whistles in my ears I catch cold or crazy or fright, I sniff it out, it's measured judged signified. I am branded. Is it your outrageous blindness or mine? Am I the enormous furious grandfather with the mad agitated little boy who've taken the subway by storm, am I this too big too old man invaded by the powerful rage of the grandson who is cross-eyed, drools, and cows the unleashed oldster? Or am I the child bent and twisted with infirmities but roused by an anger stronger than the universe? Now the giant and the fool are fighting over a packet of sweets.—Wanna the red one, screams the fool.—It is blue shouts the giant.—Wanna the red which is blue hollers the fool. The two of them come to blows. Or am I the packet of sweets, hacked in two?—It's *Reserved,* shouts the slimy child. Get off shorn Pappy, we're wrong!—Not wrong rumbles the old humus in revolt against all of life's obstacles. It's *not-* reserved! Incoercible! Lazy! A sinister story! Tortured old heart! Learn to read tumor you-die! Don't you see the *no*?—No! reverberates the deaf fool rattling all his savage apparatus, in his ears, in his eyes, in his teeth. No! No it's no no, we've wrong, horrid Pappy wrong of place wrong of time. Gimme water twisted Pappy gimme water, or I'm bust you gut on the ribs of nothing—*Give me* water! *Give me* water! Scabby old heart! Why do you say *gimme* water, punishment? Like a mountain I am gonna tip over on your good-for-nothing head like a bucket I'm gonna dump myself out, catastrophe of my tragedy. Dark jealousy of my entrails! Human throwback! Mongoloid!

Whereupon they got off in a single gianfool, clutching the torn packet. All patched up with love.

Am I on the side of *give me* water or on the side of *gimme* water? Torrent of years whipped by the screams of two damned souls over the whole of my geography. I am rolled molded reinvented. Is it an invisible odor of heart that draws the enchanted into my path?

I have just checked Adolf Eichmann's date of birth. He was born on the nineteenth of March nineteen hundred and six. What a relief. It would have infected me if his day were close to a day devoted to someone dear to me, I thought to myself. And right away it upset me to catch myself fearing being upset by it. I fear taking ill, but what I fear most is fear itself which drags me down and consents to a crime or other power of appropriation. The contagion is there, undetectable. You can't get rid of it. I still see my doctor father scrubbing his hands for ages, whipping up a blessed white foam under the tap. What detergent for what touches us by the internal contact, voluptuous, terrifying, hot coals of the mind?

It's this human porosity that bothers me and that I can't escape since it is the fault of my skin, the extra sense which is everywhere in my being, this lack of eyelids on the face of the soul, or perhaps this imaginary lack of imaginary lids, this excessive facility I have for catching others, I am caught by persons or things animated or unanimated that I don't even frequent, and even the verb *catch* I catch or rather I am caught by it, for, note this please, it's not I who wish to change, it's the other who gets his hooks in me for lack of armor. All it takes is for me to be plunged for an hour or less into surroundings where the inevitable occurs—café, bus, hair salon, train carriage, recording studio—there must be confinement and envelopment, and there I am stained intoxicated, practically any speaker can appropriate my mental cells and poison my sinuses, shit, idiocies, cruelties, vulgar spite, trash, innumerable particles of human hostility inflame the windows of my brain and I get off the transport sick for days. It isn't the fault of one Eichmann or another. I admit to being guilty of excessive receptivity to mental miasma. The rumor of a word poisons me for a long time. Should I read or hear such and such a turn of phrase or figure of speech, right away I can't breath my mucous membranes swell up, my lips go dry, I am asthmaticked, sometimes I lose my balance and crash to the ground, or on a chair if perchance one is there, in the incapacity of breathing the unbreathable.

That human phrases or even a word carry doses of maleficence is well established. People are venerated by nations for a belch or two. The poison circulates via points of resemblance or coincidence between all animated beings and more particularly by the word *I* which is in every mouth. Every time I hear someone else say I, it's the alert. Secretly I watch out I tremble I am fingered, I make myself dig a trench I am the bird aware of the hostility of the cat who is after me. But, at the same moment I am the cat aware that the bird is aware of the hostility I feel for him. It's my lot, my good fortune, and my mischance, this oscillation of other.

We are all cut out of the immense bolt of being, a dreadful kinship for someone who does not know how to put a strict limit on connivance. It's those eyelids again, this connivance. One wink, and you've reached a tacit agreement with the devil. No, no, no third lid! No hooded eye!

Therefore it is not simply that I go to the Cinema. Cinema, a vat of winking. I am still under the influence of the first film of my existence. 1942, the war, the bliss of war, the liberation of the Jews by the Allies, the joy on earth that is a beach teeming with American soldiers with Italian prisoners with liberated ruined resuscitated Jews and before my eyes night beneath the curtain of sky, a screen on which a great bustle of ghosts coming and going between here and there not the slightest difference, all the walls of the world are porous.

To the Cinema, I surrender. Fleeing, going backward, compulsively and hopeless, in the tradition of Jonah, my family ancestor, the derisory prophet, incarnation of useless recalcitrance, he who knows for nothing, the first of the Jews in general, the first of the Osnabrück Jews in particular, he who gives in and goes. But by going in the opposite direction, like all the Jonahs. This is how I go, knowing and not wanting to see, I go backward to confront the unnameable, God or the Whale. Abraham: face-to-face. But us, the Jonahs, backward. Back to front, back to life. In the saurian-smelling and bewitching viscera I take my scat on the bench of the self-accused. The court scene starts with a flourish. I spend the whole film denying any resemblance.

I went to the Cinema. Coming out of the metro I was struck with bewilderment. The staircase leads to the other world. An other. In a flash I found myself in the bright lights of the square with the church, in a daze of light. An incredible vision, this extreme crudeness of a May noon. The place: the little square, plaza of the year 1999, thronged. For the crowd, it's a Sunday to enjoy and not to think. A shower of light without a shadow. The time: It's another century. A fete was in full swing, indecipherable. A hail of scenes brief noisy in color. Nobody had three legs. It's that the people didn't remember. Everyone was dressed in colors. A Babylon organ grinder prettily done up in pink and gray plaid with a great gray cat striped pink on the side and in front a big dog and sleeping wolf tipped newcomers off to the style of the day. It is in Paris. It's not so far away, not so near either, one might expect to see hanging gardens, vines, cypresses, a camel, and a needle's eye. We find ourselves under glass and elegant as a conservatory. The beggars are tastefully dressed. Tact is in order: Do not spoil the holiday pact, its laborless mystery, "it all passed in the end it all passed," as they say, they eat crepes the café terraces multiply like loaves the restaurants extend the legs of their tables right across the streets, in the end the whole city draws up a chair and stretches out its legs, a blue-and-yellow brass band of four youths blows by the customers speak numerous languages and guzzle tall German beers. It's Berlin, but not far. As for the maîtres d'hôtel they are dressed like real maîtres d'hôtel. I see one though a little one, brown, wily looking, who is Arab. He escorts the customers to their table aboard a jeep. At the foot of the plateau, he drops them off and leaves again. Confused, the customers take a turn round the terrace on the edge of the plateau looking for the entrance. There must be steps somewhere. Around their heads an outdoor room makes the clink of forks. The city feels like a command performance. Each time a bomber flies across the scene with its nurse-plane in tow, no one is surprised. It is agreed that we are deaf. Me, head ducked because they fly so low, the son-plane and the mother-plane, I alone peek up: It's really something this pair of war gods the son ten times the size of the mother inseparable messengers of death. Mortal is what they are. The reconstitution: perfect. Immediately I pretend to do the same, otherwise people would notice. I expect to see five Jewish men with thick beards under their black hats appear on the corner of Forty-seventh Street, vaguely elsewhere as if it weren't New York but the wailing wall. They don't come along. I slip into a crack between two restaurants so obese that nothing keeps them apart except my wake breaking against the cellar door. Then I go down into 1960. The cellar extends its cavity under the floor of the buildings. In the dark one clearly feels the footsteps of people and the trotting of the waiters. From below one feels that up above people never stop walking, but on the spot, in a superimposition of dishes and terraces. No policies. Just piles.

Then I saw the film *Un Spécialiste*. A flash of pain gripped my left shoulder preventing me from turning away, and I saw everything head on, held in place by that bird of misfortune.

—If I myself had taken part in the physical extermination of the Jews, Eichmann was saying, I'd have put a bullet in my head. I think. And why? In order to find a way out of the meticulous physical situation. But I didn't have to, not being under orders to kill *glücklicher Weise*. Fortunately. Being in command of organizing the means of transport, I did not put a bullet in my head.

He nods his intact head slowly. He winks at me. He continues slowly. It's an explanation.—As a humane person I found the physical extermination of the Jonah family was a *Grässliche Sache*. A dreadful thing. That of the Engers family, also. That of the Katzman family. *Grässlich.*

In a monotonous voice he proceeds to read the list of families. I know them all. Right away I'd recognized the accent, the familiar expressions. His manner of punctuating the enunciation. These modalizations, I know them all.

—. . . but as a high-ranking government official, he adds, and he looks at me with raised eyebrows, a high-ranking military official, I followed orders. I had sworn to obey. And I had not been released from my oath. He lowers his eyebrows. Full stop. *Unglücklicher Weise.* Or rather. *Glücklicher Weise.* All these adverbial locutions, these expressions that mean nothing except that they mean it, I recognize them.

Omi always used to say *Grässlich*. I was waiting for him to say: *Um Gottes Willen.*

Right away I found him very familiar this man, this Eichmann I've known him for ages, I've met him often, he is a sincere man, crafty and sincere, one can only admire how composed his attitude is, a man who knows how to paint his own character, because he likes himself the way he is, neither more nor less than antipathetic a little abandoned, a little disappointing and therefore disappointed to have disappointed himself, but German, but still, *geputzt,* boot-licking clean, he is still handsome though fifteen or sixteen years have gone by since the events his skin is not yet wrinkled, his mouth is still neatly outlined, although he thinks he risks the death penalty, unaware as he is that being deadalready he risks nothing, and it is this deadalready and this kept under glass that make him fascinating: Here you have a dead man who doesn't know it yet. Like so many others under glass. He follows it all with attention and patience. The Obedient. Determined to be obedient. Specialized in obedience. Good in grammar. The only slip, it's that he mixed up Cholm and Chelmo which in reality is Kolm or Kolmhof but he isn't the only one who doesn't know if Cholm is Kolm or not and if yes or no it was Chelmo in the Wäthergau where he was sent to oversee some phases of extermination about which he made a report in report language to Müller his superior. The question remains in suspense.

Was he condemned to death in the end?

The question remains. . . .

My soul is lighter when I go back up to 1999, although my body is crushed and broken for having walked for so long between the tracks of the courtroom. It's that I did what I had to do that day. Descend into the cavern of my own tribunal. On the square the animated things and the populace in colors no longer bewilder me. They've been put in their place and me, I'm in my place. The clickety-clack of an old train keeps me company. Seeing this film was good for me. Each thing has come back to answer for itself. One sees clearly what is real and what is unreal. A drum roll. The whole city is off to the Great Demonstration. A hubbub of people clamber over one another in a midtown circus. Reality in the cave of the tribunal, unreality in the costume party out on the square.

What ever'd bumped and banged into me at noon when I came up from the underground and tumbled into the whale of raw light, that was the unreality of this reality which was beating its drums on the memoryless square its mouth stuffed with crepes, two hundred leagues from Kosovo or Kolmovo which did not exist before and will never exist here, not here, not now, not on the First of May 1999 day for abandoning three-legged dogs in the center of the country of Paris, capital city Berlin.

Then having thought that I began to think the opposite. My mind started to yap at the sky racing left to right to left and leaping up and down on three legs and a phantom, I shouted: What's the reality which one is the real one, who is real, who is unreal, I was screaming like the mad boy, we've wrong! Frenzied, in the throes of an abrupt loss of sight or else of street, without knowing which country which memory I am the broken habit of, am I not the rich passerby who descends between the mountains of tables heaped with food to the underside of time at full noon in the month of May in order to go and watch the oft-told tale of events which will never crush my armslegs and ventricles?

Beyond my mind, invisible, a church began to call: Jesus! Jesus! All the bells ring out a foreign tongue. A marriage? A funeral?

The First of May, day of the birth of my son the dead. Sometimes I leap to a phantom heaven.

—They are always the innocent ones, Eichmann, says my mother, there's not a thing you can do about it. He's the sort who thinks he did everything fine. You'll never convince him he's done anything wrong. It's like Pinoquet. They are poor wretches who've been accused. It never crosses his mind he did anything wrong.

—Pinochet, I say.

And right away I regret it. This mania to hold on and adjust.

But luckily my mother is safe behind the earphones of her radio. She's listening to France Culture not me.

I never think of my son the dead, I thought toward my cat who was smiling at me with her minimissimal overwhelming smile, while she watched me think on her, bearing the unspeakable mess of my mental images with the compassion that comes to her aid with my convulsions. I never think of my son the dead and that is not an exaggeration for even when he comes to mind it is not I who think of him, it is he who steals with his congenital modesty into a far corner of the room where he ends up melting away without my having made a move in his direction. He is not one to make a fuss. And even at this moment when my son the dead was the direct object of my thoughts, indirectness reigned and I did not try to curtail it. My cat leapt delicately at my nose so as to join her soul to mine in this visibly gloomy meditation. While I, I didn't budge toward my son the dead. And his nose—have I ever licked or caressed it? I could say that it's all the fault of the verb *to think;* it is because of the way it is constructed, its manner of taking an indirect object, by which it means to signify its circuitousness and precaution to us, it is a verb that prowls, a dreamy sort of action. It is a roundabout process. One must go toward the dead son and that takes time in my case it is going to take up to decades. In the old days perhaps I thought of my son directly but I do not think to remember that. Or maybe it's linked to the actualization of the verb *to think,* to the intransitiveness of its construction.

But what I see rather is that when it comes to my son I have always been indirect and vice versa, we were fated. Fate is what we have in common. Whereas *ponder* in its etymological sense, "to weigh," is transitive. But that's just it *I was never able to weigh my son,* I could not weigh him, without being caught up and overcome by an invincible terror, with the result that after a few months three or four I believe I'd given up weighing him, because weighing him for me it was as if each time I was sentenced anew, weighing him was to hear the pitiless word of the scales all over again why bother consulting them, they prophesied to me in vain, perhaps that's when I began weighing him indirectly and without noticing it became perpetual. When he reached four and a half kilos, exhausted, which I don't say to excuse myself, and besides terrorized rather than worn out, I handed him over to my mother. In order to set between us a space for thought. I gave him to my mother to weigh, without consciously knowing that I was giving my mother the whole child including the final act, exit, and epilogue.

Only to my cat, keeper of my sorrows and sentences which for me in the inside of me remain secret, can I recall this: For I do nothing else: A brief and frail evocation not much more than a flame, that is all that glimmers and remains of the vast, grave lost continent of my son the dead. Whoever has never contemplated such a flame, *the yartseit candle,* the one they would light in my family one week in February, does not know the wretched glimmer of mourning, and has never seen with his own eyes the cruel, very cruel miserly misfortune represented with a dreadful meticulousness in this very poor, very pitiful icon. One sticks a wick in a kitchen glass formerly filled with mustard filled with oil and set next to a photo of the deceased, in the form of a bad enlargement of an identity photo. I saw death in a photo: I saw death. Everything is blurred, cut, abandoned. The head is just a small portion of the body. No body. The impotence of the regretful dead. It's him, for sure. The dead's photo. The eternal flame tarnished by oil, coated alive in a film of grime. The scene is faithful in every detail to the fate of the dead. At the end of his rope, at the end of the light, at the end of looking, at the end of memory. You can tell in the distance he weighs nothing.

And so, on this First of May, without meaning to, someone had lit for me the brief, sad beam of mourning that signals the dishonoring of the dead.

It came from the family papers, the unexpected gleam. It was because I'd made a photocopy of the irreparable documents destined long since to destruction and dispersion. Compared with my grandmother's and my mother's sturdy German documents which survived the century's brutal moves, these were destined to dislocation from the very day they were fabricated. In vain does one tape the pages back into the City of Algiers's official certificates of birth and death, nothing stops the ungluing. The leaves suffered no attempt at reassembly. As I was on the point of confiding the tattered bundle to my son the wind, I had the idea of keeping some trace of a thing in its agony. And presto, up it came, good as new, a neat and tidy ghost considerably stronger than the real thing. Photocopied. As a result of this undertaking that which had been falling apart found itself together again, just like that: It told an unexpectedly modern tale, in which events make a mockery of chronological order, hence reading from west to east, I divorced on the left before bringing my daughter into the world on the right, and on the following page I suddenly saw and for the first time ever in living memory my two sons side by side preceded and thus heralded by the death sentence of my son declared dead before he was born officially.

My two sons before me together, I'd never experienced that. Side by side my two sons with death at their side, that's how they came to me. I never thought of it I thought, I never put two and two together that way, to see them lying next to one another under my eyes now, two brothers gazing up at their mother, and that happened all at once and it happened in the furthest reach of my being, it raced along my nerves with the speed of lightning, it coursed through my body like the annunciation of pregnancy, I felt the first contraction, first sign, the same as the desire for love and right away your breasts hurt and immediately came the flood of tears, the same for the shock of love when at the moment we embrace one another with the hardness of those whom the imminence of loss galvanizes we keep check on our soul abrim with thoughts which however we do not locate: We merely escape the abyss which remains agape.

Surprised, I wept. And I don't know why. Maternity rendered, maternity lost. It was for lack of thought and the fault of words

One of my sons is dead

The other is alive

How to think that

One of my sons is still alive

The other is dead

One of my sons is still dead

The other is very much alive

How to think that

My son the one who is dead, my former son my son who is no longer my son. And the one I call my son is my son the living. The other is outside, he was there for so long that I never think of him to his face.

My cat weighs four and a half kilos. I carry her around on my shoulder making sure she is holding on tight, I sing songs to her eyes.

How to ponder the weight the place the replacement the tenacity of the speechless who ask for nothing, who glimmer in a corner of your heart? How to answer the question: How many children did you have, without long, slow reflection, going back over youths and old ages, without interrogating each word of this question which interrogates me in every part of my being as if I could count up and arrive at the sum of what is still more child than child what is less child than child? You had children? Yes yes yes, how many? Oh, that! it depends. Since the apparition of my son the lamb with his webbed hands, there is an Impossibility, since the unheralded arrival of my son the Impossible, I can't say how many without the words *how many* coming undone, the child too, undone, fended off and defended and de-fended from within, how many children? That is why the day of the apparition, head turned toward the square window at which press a herd of creatures their faces a little fishlike who gaze at me through the square of glass, mouthing O, I hesitate to string together a proper sentence, with a to have and a to be in it. It's as if at the moment I was trying to answer for myself, an abrupt sensation of something missing from my mouth, and on my lap, there's a tooth. Just before I opened it, my mouth, there were thirty-two of them and at the moment I still have thirty-two of which one is no longer within but on my lap. It is small, pearly, pointy, with a black spot at the root and carved like a cat's tooth. It's my tooth which was my tooth and is no longer my tooth. I examine it.

That is what came to happen to me in the Sainte-Foy maternity home. I see the scene as if I myself were outside pressed against the windowpane my nose squashed against the glass, my mouth round with curiosity. I see it. She, that's me that day who just got tipped out of myself and no way to climb back into the house of me from which I have fallen. Time pivots and falls. There is no more past. The future not yet. What remains is a hesitation of ill-attached ill-detached present hanging over the two beds the big one and the little one. Outside the fish swim round the aquarium.

She can't get over it. She lingers in a bizarre hour, adrift, between two hours. She has just given birth, for one thing. For another, what has happened it's that the one who has just been born, he hasn't quite yet arrived anywhere, he is not in his place, he wriggles weakly still in the wings, offstage as if detained by a tremendous uncertainty, as if timid. As for her she doesn't move, she waits. For the place. She doesn't think: What a surprise this child, this child which doesn't seem to be hers, who differs, who doesn't look like, this fish gasping as if it needed to go back in the water, one expects a surprise but instead of the expected surprise it's an entirely different one, O mysterious power of the new arrival who upsets the millions of expectations of millenniums of images, O eternally astonishing natural phenomenon forever never seen before. And this one here, he's the champion. He evades her absolutely, she doesn't remember him at all. She doesn't conceive of him. She has come to a stop. Where? At the stop.

I see the woman do silent battle with the child, this is in one of those worlds where on the threshold a spell is cast over whoever strays or ventures in, where the laws of metamorphosis reign, where one never knows who pursues whom for dozens of light-years, where one cannot not hunt as one breathes. I see the woman and child beasts, held alive in the burning frost of a face-to-face the way two cats caught in the last two meters of a kingdom stand still for hours guarding the last two meters with the patient tenacity of gods measuring out between them their last chance at immortality.

The way two heroes advance toward the final instant slowly sharing the taste of each inch of white sand, which is what they have in common, this morsel of earthly fabric which kisses their feet, they do not run they revel together in what unites them in a loving hostility, this space which is not going to last, which they are going to cut, unequally, this solemn diminution.

They stare at one another, distractedly, that's what's strange.

The woman glances out of the corner of her eye at the face of the one who has just arrived, oblique. Then she jerks her head away as if fearing some danger, darts a glance in the direction of the window on the other side of which the bizarre spectators are pressed together, then brings all her power of inquiry to bear on the face of the child. On his face is an absence. Something unfocused maybe. A kind of veil. You couldn't say she dotes on him. She bends an ear. She tries to make out what the sentences are whispering to her, rushing past like sighs.

It's that there is something in the back of her mind that she can't quite grasp yet she feels a form devoid of strength flit by or on the contrary a form monstrously strong in its weakness. The vague child. At the pane the crowd presses in.

A sentence says: "What has just happened" and she hears the strangeness of this *what*.

What has happened is that the child in the cradle has not arrived yet, at least he hasn't been informed. He believes he is drifting, he hasn't yet landed. "What has come to pass." How to describe it, how to describe, this to come which has already come and which is still on the way, which hasn't finished, which isn't finished, which doesn't commence, which is all mixed up. Because if *this* has happened, it has happened but if it is still coming it's that *this* hasn't happened, which is what renders the child still intangible though in the cradle. Morphologically it's a present, but curved, melting, receding. Missing. The child has arrived, incorrect.

The woman's heart beats slowly. The child's heart beats excessively fast. This isn't it. This is not where it is. *This* is not there.

All of a sudden she thinks something crazy: He isn't born. Does it exist, to be born without being born yet? To be almost? Almost.

On the eve of the day she gave birth she was reading *The Idiot*. Reality is a fabulous book in which everything happens when one least expects it. Everything that has never existed explodes into being from one page to the next. Fantastic plot. Chapter 7. I'm a prince. Flight. Enter the monster. Take me back home. It would have been better to nip me in the bud. A trifle. Better yet: to nip me before the bud. To have only a few months to live is this living? What is the length of that we call life? Sunrise, and the other world. One doesn't understand a thing. Being nothing, I still want. One can't not love. One doesn't know what it means to love. I see the woman bending over herself. What she calls love beats very slowly. Then suddenly excessively fast. Then very slowly.

Now she takes sides, the side of the child. The side of the vague.

She calls him.

She puts her hope in the name. She is going to catch the slippery little fish in the net of names she casts over him. Then he will turn into a little boy which is what he has not yet managed to be. She will trap him in the net of very old, strong, safe, faithful names, her secret and sacred names, and she will pull him gently out of the invisible water he has drawn around himself up to his chest.

First she calls him Adam; second she calls him George the name of her dead father who had been waiting for years to be called back among the living. Third she calls him Lev for the complicated, inexplicable Prince.

For the fourth she stops, for already she has mustered an entire army around the little boy.

She calls him.

The names are good for him. Their infinitesimal wings flutter in his ears. She has the feeling the baby is sending her tiny sounds of names soft to her ears. It's that now he's called. Now Adam, now George, now Lev. It's good for him to have such strong names, it's a whole story surrounding him, stretching far back, now he is told, he has hardly not been out his cradle she lifts him up, now he has a character, the wind blows, a diluvian storm slams into the building the weird bunch of creatures in O is swept away, firmly she holds the head of her son which is so ponderous. It is in danger of falling off, it's the neck which is awfully flexible she rocks him in her arms.

What strikes her is the lack of meanness on the extraordinarily peaceful face. It makes no sense. A mad confidence is manifest. Next to the face of her son all the newborn faces project a sour little something, a little line of defense, a scribble, a grimace. He is smooth, abstract. As if he hadn't risen. Pale, as if he hadn't finished baking.

A Nose Newborn?

Or maybe *the nose is the question,* a new noseborn in the family, which for noses always had the idea of a fin or a prehistoric flipper standing like a monolith in the middle of a delicate and well-trimmed field. See the photos of my father, with a rudder plumb in the middle.

Noticing this one-of-a-kind nose, without ancestor, without length, without idea, she feels it holds the key to the strangeness: "What has been born to me, as if it had acceded to the objurgations of generations of my family up in arms one after another against the old nose," she thought audacious and troubled, "can it be a sort of non-Jew?" The blond hair the paleness as well, a son come from elsewhere, curtailed.

"I didn't want that," she murmured to the strict and taciturn presence of her father. And yet. "It's the rest of the family, who wanted it. Who can fathom the mysteries of creation? All of us in the family we fought over the blue blue eyes of Omi my grandmother and finally it's a great grand-nephew in Australia who got them, Mendel's laws say one thing, people do something else, one doesn't give orders to the unconscious, God is an active volcano, species are reduced to ashes, new features arise, new words, new diseases, new planets, new princes, new misfortunes."

My nose and I we have a vital relationship, a fated relationship, to which I can compare no other relation unless it is the relation with my inseparable lover. Every part of me is in keeping with this exterior and interior element of my being, everything is determined by it, for it is the only element or the only part of my vital whole which I have considered parting with. I was tempted to do it and finally after more than a year of temptation I gave up the idea of dissociating myself from it. On the subject of my nose I served the better part of my apprenticeship to good and evil, to loyalty and treason, to baseness and courage, to the mortal illness of the soul and solitude, to the lack of imagination and autoimmunity, to the proximity of the destruction of the interior treasure, and to self-hate, to the fragility of the sense of right choice and the power of attraction of the mortal enemy, to the astonishing facility with which we come to terms with those who wish us ill and whom we go out of our way to help, to the scorn we do not hesitate to inspire in ourselves, to the childish naïveté that lets us wade into shit and poison ourselves, to the complacency with which we give ourselves over to the usurpation of our own beauty. I stop.

"Get a nose job," said my matter-of-fact mother when I arrived at the age of puberty, for it seems that this is when one has one's definitive nose. And I nearly. And I failed. I had just turned fourteen and I translated my nose into a thing for cutting, a thing of shame, a flag of ugliness flying over my countryside, into something disgusting to be got rid of. Then for a few years I didn't stop nearlying now on one side now on the other. Tugged this way and that between my father underground with his big nose and my matter-of-fact mother, for whom a nose is just a nose. Years of internal strife, wars, accusations, and denials that I never stopped bringing against myself in one way or in the other.

Finally I spared my nose that I really should have liked to cut off, but I didn't dare, for a cut nose doesn't ever grow back again, I learned that from Aeschylus.

Nose cut, terminated, once blood is spilled in the dust it doesn't rise in the veins again, that nose there, my inheritance, my father, I don't want to part with it, my father's ghost haunted me and spoke not a word, which condemned me to a difficult liberty.

I was afraid of cutting myself off from my father.

Not that my mother'd got it wrong. For two or three years I never went out with my nose naked, I went through the streets of Algiers with my nose under the fingers of my left hand as if I were trying not to sneeze, I kept it out of sight.

Lots of the things I think or act go back to my nose. Mostly negative.

Nor can one simply say that I didn't cut it off. During my Nez Caché period it was as if I cut it off to go out and stuck it back when I returned to my room. I put back the cut and the join each in turn, and I couldn't see where the crisis would end.

It was pure luck that I still had my nose when I left Algeria. Today we are reconciled, one thing is forgiven, but nothing is forgotten. It's peace head on but not in profile.

—It's all Hitler's fault, says Aunt Eri my mother's sister. We do whatever he wants without meaning to.—But me when I was over there I didn't know Hitler and you didn't either says my mother.—It's that there wasn't any television, we'd never seen Hitler, says my aunt, one didn't see him. —But me when I came to visit Omi in 1933 says my mother, my uncle, and all the gentlemen of the consistory, they were in jail, "for their own protection." But nobody'd seen Hitler. There was always a *gesunder Antisemitismus* as they used to say, says my aunt, but one got along very well with this *Antisemitismus*. Only one time I had a problem because I had my nose done. I went to see *den Nasenjosef,* he was very famous, the Joseph-of-Noses, because I had this big nose. Now there was an anti-Semitic paper and in the paper it told about a girl from Osnabrück that she'd had *den Synagogenschlüssel* redone. That was in the paper *der Wächter* and the one who'd had the key to the synagogue trimmed it was me. *Dann haben sie genau gewusst.* It's a small town and people knew exactly where the key was. Me I was disgusted. And mostly embarrassed. And you couldn't complain. After when my daughter had a big nose that she didn't want, she couldn't go and see the *Nasenjosef,* who had been deported, but there was his successor. There was still the *Antisemitismus.* And the big noses we always had them fixed, and the children of the children's noses too even when there is no anti-Semitism.

—Hitler, says my aunt, I thought it's only a year and it's not going to last. But the big nose doesn't just last for a year.

—The Jews, says my mother, were more racist than the racists, but you can't say it, says my mother. With the Poles the German Jews who had a very good position, of course one felt superior.—It is always the poor Poles who came, says my aunt.—No need to spit in our own soup, says my mother.—But I'm not spitting, says my aunt. We always gave them money.—*Ne! Ne!* Not money, says my mother, train tickets. There were always pogroms in Poland. They were a motley bunch, who turned up on our doorsteps, moaning and groaning about how miserable they were. They would come to the consistory. The consistory would give them a train ticket for the next town. Don't repeat it. One mustn't spit on one's own name. Still there was a feeling of caste, or class. Already Frau Engers, although she wasn't Polish, she would talk very loud, she didn't have good manners.—And the Ehrlichs?—Them too. We didn't associate with them.—Horst Engers, says my aunt, he came to see us. I spoke to him, but I didn't invite him. Not just the people of Polish origin nobody associated with them. So in this little German community there were castes. Frau

Engers too who didn't have good manners. Those big families who had the big stores, they were Omi's school friends and vice versa. The school friends it was the big families who had the big stores.

—There was another group, that was the lawyers. They didn't mix with the *Kaufleute,* the merchants. Only Omi crossed the line with Frau Engers who made hats however but she had a small business and her husband was only a traveling salesman for pharmaceutical and Dutch products.

This friendship between two people 100 percent different and also the background not being the same, only Omi could do that. Says my mother.

Children were seen and not heard at table in the best families. Except us, Omi's children. Aunt Hete blames her that the children we speak at table. But Omi tells her sister: So who do I speak to then? There were even castes at table. But that doesn't go out of this room, says my mother.

AND NOW LOOK WHAT HAS COME TO PASS in this Maternity room, only a few years after the nose crisis, a child with the key to the synagogue sawn off at birth, will wonders never cease. Adam? She murmurs. All the while musing on the semantic ghost of the verb *to come* in its role of ancillarized auxiliary, it's that he hasn't yet come into being, he who is come. She too begins to dissolve a little in the room, a distancing of herself misting her, yesterday was in another time, the join won't take, the relationship between her and Adam of the pug nose who bears the name of George her father growing stronger with every moment, everything is farther away and everything is closer than everything, they are under the influence.

Or is it maybe that it's the cut, the impossible cut with her father that has finally at long last taken place?

"George" she murmurs, "George" she bursts out, it's the first time she calls the name of her dead father, "George!" George gives a feeble blink of his feebly slanted eyes, coming back from having come from afar.

What could be less improbable—the Wheel of Time spins on its axis, here comes the Absentee.

I don't know how many children I had. *If* I *had* some how many I have. Kept, lost, put away, eaten up. And how many I may still have, find, lose abandon especially, refuse to have them in my house but not in my heart of hearts. How to add up the living and the dead, the ephemeral and the enduring. Neither addition, nor subtraction, nor succession. I never mention my son the dead to avoid any misunderstanding for if it is more or less true that one of my sons is deceased, he is none the deader for that, it is truer that I never had nor lost my elder son. The truth of the matter is neither recognizable nor thinkable, nor separable from me. He is hardy, he is mixed into my circulation, he is entwined with my roots, forgotten to my memory, furtive, barely sketched, what remains is his wilted smile, his portrait jaundiced at birth, growing yellower and yellower, as the months went by, for he ate nothing but carrots. That too was a surprise, a chagrin, and relief: nothing but carrots and never a drop of any milk. As long as I tried to feed him milk as a child like any other, he brought it all up, all milk was a threat of death. Mother's milk cow's milk powdered milk Nestlé milk, Pelargon milk, poison milk, assassinated with milk. When he had no more skin on his buttocks nor on his back, the flesh peeled off, flayed, him dangling by needles to the drip, my horrible-to-contemplate larva, a baby bunny hunted down by his family which orders the worm to about-face I no longer knew whom to want to die me too pinned to the pinup, and nostalgia for the placental time when without blows and wounds we were one and the same blood.

I have a son and another son. The one who talks and the one to whom I have never said I. Already in the room in Sainte-Foy, he is the-one-who-is-not-there, in person. Of all my children he is the only no-one-in-person. The family hero. The key to my interior synagogue, the director of my faith. All without a word. The simple saint. And my breasts bound till the milk dries up. When I understood that the infant blithely given the name of George, and Adam, and Lev, was my unconscious loss, my loss of consciousness, and that that loss was the key to my life, and that I was twenty-two, I set out. Me and the Absentee, his pale and yellow little impersonage.

— This infant has mongoloid features says the Catholic pediatrician on his way out.

— That? It's a mongolian. Better to put him out of his misery, your little patient, you'll see. A vegetable. At best an animal. I've got one in the building. Can't keep his head up. I attached it to a plank, says the Jewish pediatrician to the midwife my mother.

Eve our mother looks up the mongolian in the dictionary. It's her first. Thus Asia the immemorial comes back.

From Tatar, Ulaanbatar, small bare-backed horses faster than the wind gobble up the fat of the steppes mixed with little children whose cheeks are rubbed red and their gallop has just flickered out panting behind the square window of Sainte-Foy. The Tatar sorcerers and sorceresses croak at the slant-eyed window. From very far they had smelled seen the odor of us and ours. They want to sing:

Chorus of Mongolians
We the mongolians
If a mother lifts us up
In her arms she holds the supernatural continents
On the map you won't find us
She is lifting God's trial-pieces
We the mongolians we look like God and like nobody, neither ugly nor mean we are orphans we belong to no parent
Mongolian to mongolian we repeat ourselves.
These days no one says *mongolian* anymore,
Mongolian, it's not a nice word. *Down's syndrome* is better, less notice-able, less crude, less believed and believing, it's more scientific and less god.
—*Down's syndrome, preferred medical terminology.* Henceforth there are no more mongolians.
We are mummified silkworms in an abandoned cocoonery on the road to Ulaanbaatar. We are larval angels crusting the rungs of the ladder sunk in the bottom of the Dead Sea.
On the paper our letters washed away by the storm
Who will read the message?
When? When ever?
If a mother lifts us to her lips in tears
We cry—an!—an! and at best—man!

In Algeria during the World War, there was also a substitution in 1940 and in correct terminology on the part of sensitive souls, not Jews but from one day to the next it was *Israelites preferable,* instead of Arab *preferred terminology indigenous peoples,* instead of "I want" better to say "I should like."

We the mongolians if somebody stares at us
We make them yearn for the lost country
Stones carved in the homeland in the days of God
Our eroded faces resemble the face of time passing
Promising age with its furrows
We are the vaguely children without schoolbags. At the door to the

schoolhouse which everyone enters except for us, we wave our webbed hands

Around the air where the silver ball slips from our grasp, for us the ball goes too fast we wake too late to catch it alive still, we are sick about that.

But if someone dead is buried in the family we do not keep his soul from returning to roost in our gills, for we have no right (or wrong) age. We are nice nice nice!

He's an emperor without dominion, an emperor who draws from his misery of human rabbitry an absolutely enigmatic empire exercised over any person who ever once lifts him up off the ground. Should an unwary person take him in her arms, right away a spell is cast over her. The attachment is worse than a magic potion. Some innocent vampire hides in this rabbit: the absolute authority of the rabbitlamb born for the sacrifice and who asks nobody where the lamb is that will take his place. But it's a lamb that can't stand on its own feet. Bumpety-bump up the Moriah slope, it's a long steep climb. How many years?

One year and fifteen days more or less.

But naturally starting out one doesn't know when and how it's going to end, this trial. Everything having been already decided, all one has to do is keep on, slowly and surely, to the finish, without an idea and without an opinion.

Besides when the infant George was already deceased and buried in the Saint-Eugene Jewish Cemetery, my son remained alive as long as the news of the event hadn't reached me, which took place just before the birth of his brother, my living son. "Two weeks ago," says my mother, turning up on the dot for the next one. About a fortnight ago, ten days or fourteen does it matter, one is at the crossroads, dead already alive still a little less dead than dead, but for the record preferred terminology: *deceased*. Right after the news my son the following takes his place in the shredded booklet. But even then. Until this morning I never read those papers. I had never read the news. There was no date.

Death does not interest my mother the midwife. The news of the disappearance of persons close to her does not reach her.

—Omi's brothers and sisters who disappeared in the concentration camp, when did you hear?

She has no idea.

—The death of little George?—What can I say?—But you were there? She never manages to have been there. Years later, the death hasn't happened yet. Maybe never. Death exists? She'd rather not know.

Letter to my son to whom I have never written a letter

My love, to whom I have never declared my love,

I write in the house I had built because of you, in haste for you and against you while Eve our mother was looking after you, I was building I wasn't writing anymore, instead of poems, I was building I responded to your arrival with stones for the time of times, I welcomed you, I fended you off, in haste I raised a house to hold us and to keep us apart, I built the house to which you have never come. A house finished on 1 September 196– on the day you too were done.

I never think of the origins of this house born of your birth. When I knew your name overnight I ceased to write.

I write in this house that I built never to write again.

I inherited this house in which I write to you about your interminable passage.

I'll thou you, I'll conjure you, I'll lure you from your hidden nest.

In this brief truce of an I'll, I'll take in my arms the ghost of the flayed lamb.

As I was writing I felt his cheek grate against my lips.

—Well, that one won't be needing the *Nasenjosef* says my aunt.

—He looks a little strange to me says my mother. I asked a friend of yourfather, a Jewish pediatrician. At the time I hadn't a clue.

—It's a mongolian, I'm saying it to you, but don't tell the family.

—It's not the sort of thing you say. All mongolians look alike. Another embarrassment. So I said: It's my grandson and the friend never got over his anger at me.

All these distinctions, says my mother, Jews too, they make distinctions.

The word: *distinction*. Omi was very distinguished. Right up to George's birth, she was the most distinguished member of the family. How does one distinguish distinction? And now, the one who's distinguished, it's my son the mongolian. But Omi came from such a good family she was admitted to the lodge of woman Freemasons, even if she was friends with Frau

Engers. She was well brought up but it didn't bother her that Frau Engers wasn't well brought up. The German Jews with the Polish Jews, one feels superior, it always bothered me this feeling of caste, I was already for Europe in 1925 with Fraulein von Längeke our German teacher but afterward what bothered me most it's when the Nazis started giving the impression of making the same distinctions but of course that was just a pretense. The consistory was in prison but they thought only Polish Jews were deported as if they were more Jewish for being Polish and they more German albeit Jewish thus both more and less Jewish at once.

And only dogs with three legs are abandoned on the First of May who being cut dogs are less than dogs therefore no longer dogs and more obviously abandonable.

But all this depends on how you look at it and is secondhand.

—Right away I have two options, I see them clearly says my mother, either to kill him or adopt him. Kill him I couldn't bring myself, they are poor children all the same who are rarely autonomous, if they want to live they can't, you have to force-feed them, try milk after milk until you arrive at carrots, if they want to run about their whole body makes them tumble down, if they want to die we keep them alive, you are always pushing in the opposite direction, keeping their heads above water with a plank, all the same it's a shame at the time of George yourfather you had to die whereas these days they keep old ladies going who are not all there any-more. You kill the child for the mother's sake, afterward you blame your-self for it. I was afraid you'd ask me questions, says my mother, asking me when he died or of what how and that I would get all muddled up in your questions which always tack another question on to the question, I was afraid to let the cat out of the bag, I was afraid you'd blame me for it one day, something that I'd done wrong meaning to do right, kill, lie, or on the contrary that you wouldn't ask any questions which would have kept me hanging indefinitely.—Besides I wouldn't have done it because a child that's alive one can't just do away with it, says my mother, therefore I didn't have the possibility, only the idea might have crossed my mind, added my mother, as if years had gone by while she was talking and brought every-thing she might have thought sliding down like sand.

In which I see the lunar influence of my son whose presence of absence has always caused such swings of thought. Everything that slips and slides in us, it's him, my fallen-out-of-the-nestling.

—In the end, each time I had the chance to kill one of my loved ones in order to do the right thing, I didn't have the courage for fear of blaming myself either for or against, which is how I didn't have the courage to kill Omi when the time came, when she no longer had her wits about her only a pair of eyes which, seeing nothing in the end, kept after me with a blue that had never been more terribly blue already she was no longer there and I'd apologize to her eyes, all I wanted was for her to hurry up and die but that is a thing no one can admit to themselves but I might have wished it without meaning to, wished that she would stop dying by degrees and suffering, that she would grow weak enough, except that Omi had a heart to withstand all of our wishes, and today still I blame myself for this impossible indecision. My fear was to lie that I was giving her the death that she no doubt would have asked for if she'd still had her wits about her, when perhaps all I was doing was freeing myself from her needless suffering. One burden I cannot bear, I go up to the bed and I hear Omi moaning, it's a crime, to hear the moans of one's own mother and not hear them is also another crime, and to be in her room when she is no longer there except the eyes with their obstinate blue capable of facing up to even her new-found blindness, that too is a crime, the bag of peepee too, it is all crime, and not a word, not a gesture, so as not to commit yet another crime. And for the baby instead of moans, those quick, stifled little snorts due to his cardiac malformation you remember how he always seemed to be in a rush or as if running away, as if he was running in his cradle before or ahead of or after—was that the birth, the day? The squashed-up creature gives the impression of something so forsaken, especially when after swimming in urine he no longer has his skin to protect him, and even so you are the one who abandons him, you don't want to hear him rattle anymore, it's a feeling of desire so sickening that it would be a relief to have him stop his moaning, not to have to listen to him moan anymore, Omi, the baby, and that is why I couldn't, afraid of giving myself their death in giving them the death which however they had truly merited, bothered I was doing it for myself, as if I were sneaking something out of your cupboard, which I have never done, and I didn't give anything since I couldn't see how to get round myself, I was afraid to feel let out of prison and relieved.

Inversely for the baby, cried my mother, in a voice that was swollen with indignation, it never occurred to me to kill it, it was always our mascot and I'd never have been able nor want to nor have wanted to be able to either nor have wanted to want to be able to either even to think of putting it to death. That idea therefore can only come from you.

—But—I began my sentence and no one will ever know what my sentence would have said for it was cut off by a fishtail, by my mother's taking the bend in the road without a glance to the side, something that she has started doing lately. As if drunk with some emergency on her tail and whispering reckless maneuvers. She bolted, leaving behind any other narration than this one, any version which might have preceded today's being obliterated, rendered null and void by the clauses of this new will.

Sitting on the side of the road I watched her gallop the tale with stupefied admiration, raising in her passage a cloud of white dust which settled over the preceding pages and blanked them out. The violence of her conviction sent me reeling. What if I was the one who'd invented this whole business of suppression, and it was I who wronglyremembered clearly having heard her tell me: I thought of killing him but I didn't dare. I hesitated. We do not possess ourselves, and we are all possessed, I am absolutely sure that my mother told me the thing in question and without any fuss, but I wouldn't swear to it. In any case I would never let myself swear that what someone told me in secret had really been said by that someone especially if it's a question of my mother or my lover, at least swear it to a third party, knowing full well that one can trust no unconscious, all the more so when one unconscious is in communication with another unconscious.

—*There too,* my mother cried out, I blamed myself for not having given him a shot to alleviate his suffering and shorten his life, a stupidity, for which one suffers for no reason at all. It's a kind of crime in reverse, it's an obligation not to do whatever one feels the obligation to do. At which point that woman who comes to certify the death asks me: "Did she die of natural causes?" At ninety-five years old. I ask you. In fact I had no idea with what. Besides Omi had asked: Give me something. At ninety-five I've lived long enough. I'm tired of it. Before falling. Before she fell. She still had her mind. Give me something and don't tell me about it. Give. But what? Who to ask? Ask to give what? You have no one to confide in. You haven't confidence in anyone. There's no one. I never have anyone to talk to. And that's why I didn't answer Omi. She would have been spared two falls and two operations which were totally useless to arrive at the same point. The only person I had confidence in.

The only person my mother had confidence in was her mother, and Omi had told her: *Give but don't tell me.* It was not I. It's not impossible that Omi may have thought that her daughter had given her; given without telling. According to my mother this hypothesis is to be ruled out, Omi never thought that my mother had given her *something* because she wanted not to know, one prefers not to know says my mother, Omi never knew according to my mother that is what she wanted because she wanted to stop living but without this being dying, being lucid and strong enough to be afraid of what the whole world is afraid of, and when the time came Omi was no longer in any state to know whether my mother had given or not and everything was too late. What remained was suffering and for no reason. While according to me Omi might have thought that my mother would never tell her and she could have received without acknowledging what my mother hadn't given her, so that even without having given anything, my mother had nonetheless given Omi something. But my mother assures me that this hypothesis is my invention. According to her Omi knew that my mother wasn't going to do it otherwise she would have ordered her to do it, but she had only asked her to keep it secret. Say what you like, Omi was afraid of the mystery and so was my mother, says my mother.

At the end the only presence she had was in the hand with which she squeezed my mother's hand.

—She had a heart that didn't stop beating, she hadn't eaten a bite for ages, she had lost her mind long ago, only her heart thump-thumped she was just an organ. But when I gave her my hand her hand squeezed my hand. The doctor said: That's just a mechanism. So even the hand, I didn't give it to her perhaps. Why shorten the life that is no longer anything but a mechanism says the doctor? There's nothing to give. It's going to stop all by itself. I thought completely the opposite. Between the doctor and midwife it's always war says my mother. The doctor always has to get it wrong the midwife has to shut up.

There too I blame myself says my mother.

—Why do you say *there too*? I say.

—I didn't say *there too* says my mother. I said: I blame myself for not having lightened her life. She didn't want to pee in her bed. Every half hour she had to get up. I told her but go in your bed, you have a diaper. I was afraid she'd fall. No says Omi all my life I never peed in my bed. At the end I got the little Chilean cousins Inès and Nancy for the nights because me I'd had enough of getting up every half hour, give me something says Omi, she doesn't see very well, she only wants me, she's not interested in battling with pee for her life. And that's exactly why I didn't give her: because unfortunately I was sick and tired of getting up. Omi was just the heart and the hand she kept giving me. And to conclude if I had put an end to her days naturally I wouldn't have confided in anyone. But I didn't do it. Only Omi knows. Besides I am incapable of knowing how I would have managed to get round yourbrother the doctor's vigilance when I was even tempted to ask him to help me put her to sleep, but you can't ask a doctor any of that sort of thing even when it's only a doctor you can ask for that sort of remedy. Because even so one doesn't want to kill oneself. Merely rock them to sleep. How could he have burdened his doctor's conscience with that? Only he could answer. And if Omi could have spoken at the end, do I know what she would have told me? My mother-in-law always used to say: Do what's best and forget the rest, she would say that in Oran, but if you examine the sentence everything gets twisted around, as if you know what's best what's rest. I see very clearly that *I was caught between the devil and the deep blue sea,* says my mother. One never does the right thing, one does one's best but it's not good. Him too, the baby, I held onto him in spite of everything. He seemed to me a boy who would have been intelligent. But it was just an idea I had, as his mother I always thought he wouldn't have been too stupid, says my mother.

—You said: "A boy who would have been intelligent" I shouted but in a low voice so as not to frighten her away but to slow her down, wait, wait, I wanted to hear those words, I held my hand up to make her stop. Whoa! the Algiers carter used to say to his horse and me I say Whoa! to my mother.

—Not at all my mother corrects herself immediately and her eyes grow round with thinking she's said something stupid, it was just an idea I had in which I didn't believe, she protests. An absurd fleeting image in the future which would not exist and right away her daughter latches on to it. But what I wanted to hear again that is to have truly heard it wasn't the idea, it was that word: *boy.* For if there is one word which never came to mind with George around, a word that never lit fluttering on the lip of the cradle it was *boy.* With all the words and names there was no *boy.* It's the first time I trembled, that I've heard it spoken: Hence for my mother he had in the end but in the secret of her innermost, most hidden thoughts become the sketch of a boy. He was a real *mongolian* my mother hastens to say but once when I was alone, the idea came to me, like a shimmer of a thought, an illusion which you would be mortified to have become public knowledge. For a moment we bent together over the word *boy.* And my mother with a jolt was off again.

—*Being extremely good-natured* he had lots of mothers. I shall list the entire Staff, among which first of all the nurses' aides, Kheira, Barta who washed the floors, next the midwives first Kenous, the red-haired one, the one who met a handsome French officer at the hospital, they fell for each other then he went back to his wife in France, and the one who was from the South, a Mozabite who really had been trained but in England, a good midwife, who had come at her request to take her place. She turns up and the Kabyle one tells her no I'm staying, I don't need a replacement. I've changed my mind, she was carrying George in her arms and *there was an attachment.* What's going on here? shrieks the Mozabite from England. I tell myself: I'll pay her, too bad if the other one wants to stay, she's attached. You get paid and you don't do the work I say, even though she was a good midwife. She shouts: You're going to pay me and I'll work nights, and Kenous didn't want to leave the baby and says: I'm staying. The other one shouts: I'm replacing you. I say: It doesn't help to shout. She shouts: Hah! but me I need to shout. She was very smart. Later she became a big shot in the South. The other one, the red-haired one, she'd lost her marbles. You'd have thought George had an influence. No need of a beverage: the baby. Another one, Rozouk—the one who wouldn't let you into the delivery room—no! nobody enters. She had a habit, she used to cut. As soon as a woman is in labor. She cuts her up. But why are you cutting? Try not to, I say.—It's what I'm used to. Me I cut says Rozouk. But with George, she would carry him around on her back. The other one too, the worst of all, Kayouche, each time there was a delivery we got there in the nick of time and one day I caught her playing with George, even though she was such a terror. He was the toy. Everyone was disarmed. At the Clinic all the midwives and the Staff, he was their mascot. A two-bit saint, peace all around him, without doing it on purpose, everyone who came near him went off in their own opposite direction. Me too, my mother goes on. What complicated matters, it was that at the time I took the baby I had a friend it upset that people got attached to those sorts of children. He left me at the time because he too was growing attached to the baby. I had him for several months and everybody grew attached to him. One doesn't notice it, and all of a sudden, without him being able to do a thing about it, this child attaches you. My friend said he didn't want to get attached to a child like that because one gets attached to these nice children and *one can't ever get unattached again.* He was intelligent and you never heard a word of complaint from him. My friend the opposite. At seven months he was toilet trained. Not good-looking but not too ugly. A baby you gave food and drink to. It bothered my friend this beginning of an attachment. I had a colleague who got married four times. At the time she had a husband who was a doctor. She had started a maternity home in the entryway of a corridor. She was *the initiator*. Always she wanted to initiate me. She told me: The biggest piece of fruit, it's always in my dish. You think that's luck? As if it fell out of the tree into my dish. I'm going to give you the trick. Always she wanted to initiate me. How did she make it work the home in the corridor entry? You go to the old folks' home, says the initiator. There are lots of old women who are abandoned who are still good for something and ask for nothing more. She'd got an old woman with her face all wizened up but tough, she did *everything*. One day the old woman says to me, says my mother: I make a good living, and she, the initiator, she puts *it* all aside for me. The Fruit of her labor. I think of this old woman who never saw a penny, says my mother. She was a capable woman with her inconsistent nursing home. She was right not to do any sort of delivery she hadn't learned to do, being originally a secretary. She did abortions, it's what she did best. At the time she was on her third husband, a young man twenty years younger than she is, a prison guard. She always used to say to him: when we have children. What's she on about, I would think, she can't have children, she's fifty years old already, and no uterus anymore either, but at least he never lost hope—have children, and have hope it's already like having children in your head. She used to concoct potions. She says to me I'm going to initiate you. I'm going to show you a drink. She says to me: I'm going to give you potions to keep your friend attached, says my mother. I said: no thanks. Or else we get married because we want to. If he doesn't want I'm not going to force anyone says my mother.—At least get rid of the child, says the initiator. Exactly what she shouldn't have said to me, says my mother. That child wasn't going to last. What scared my friend was the attachment. It's no good to force things. At the time he left me not to get attached because he was getting attached. *Who knows why things happen?* my grandmother used to say, says my mother. *Gam su letouvo?* If it's wrong you can't know it's not right. *Gam su letouvo* is written however you like, if it's written wrong you can't know it's not right and vice versa. Probably I was wrong all the same but maybe not. I could have sent the child back to its mother, that is to you. But had I done so I should have been bound to send my friend away too. Morally.

There were other reasons as well: One time I'd made crepes one evening when the friend came for dinner, and one was bigger. Crepes with jam. Me out of politeness I didn't take the big one. He asks me: Why do you take the small one? I say: To be polite I give you the biggest. He says: What did you put in it? I say jam. He thought I'd put one of those aphrodisiacs you concoct with toenails and hair. I know what women get up to, says he. And he didn't eat the crepe. I told myself: If it's not to be, it's not to be. And I ate the crepe. After which he left me a little before he died. In the end I don't know whether I didn't push him more because of the crepes or because of George. But if I hadn't made crepes with jam that evening, or on the other hand if I had made crepes the same size and then if he hadn't left me at the time thinking I wanted to attach him either with remedies or with those sorts of children that one can't get rid of afterward, and a little while after the crepes there's George dead, would he have married me? Without being scared of *an attachment*? I wonder. Still I thought it might be a solution. I was extremely fond of him. He was very nice. It was better he die. Keep him alive by force, no thanks. What will be will be, God provides, even if you, you don't see, as my grandmother used to say, says my mother.

SO YOU WANT TO KNOW THE END? says my mother. Yes, I say. Up till then we'd never spoken of the end, I don't know for what reasons, and that day, as if it had traversed a sea of silence and earth tunneling through time, the day of the end of this suspense that had gone on for years and years, was coming, had just come. I did not know the date of my son George's death, I who each year receive the visit of George my father at ineradicable and shining dates. I note that never having asked any questions I do not know that the child is dead: He has only changed absences. For her part my mother'd never had the need or the idea of telling me about it. But the whole life of this child has always taken place before the invention of the story, it wasn't ready to be told, I tell myself, while my mother remained silent, the final silence, I thought. Always there'd been this time lag in our time, things, in the life of my son, taking much more time to happen than in the time of our lives off to the side, ripen, die, everything took its time, on the one hand he never stopped making us wait for him, as if restrained by the mystery of some slowness, on the other hand beneath this slowness brooded an extreme rapidity but a rapidity of another sort than ours, as if in his region which can be called his Asia, an immense unexplored region but not forbidden to my contemplation, life was governed by rhythms and precipitations which always caught me off guard. Youth, adolescence, maturity, the ages, all his seasons completely other than ours. When he was seven months old, the age at which he gave my mother the satisfaction of being able to believe that, coinciding with a standard child, he did his business as my mother said on a real potty, he swam in my eyes very below the surface, I saw him leading his life in great glaucous depths which didn't keep him from winking an eye at us or nudging what would later be a smile toward the crack in his lips, and while I watched him evolving in this space made up of proximate distances, his face struck me for its gravity of another age as if he were watching me from the top of an antique column as I evolved beneath his eyes in an area comparable to a foreign language. United in a single incomprehension we shared gropingly. And all unsayable. A sort of ancientness in his expression.

—All right, says my mother, now, I'm telling you *the end:*

When she got to husband number four, it was a Spanish dancer, and she was crazy about him. But the family tells her you're mad, what an idea to go to Spain! He offered her jewels. So the family tells her just keep the jewels. And that's what she did. She kicked him out. Just when a woman she'd put a probe in died. She was scared of the vengeance. So she left for France. And that was the last I heard of her. Says my mother mentally counting down the ten steps of this departure.

And the end is that there was a midwives' meeting in Monaco and a midwife told me: You won't believe it! Mrs. D. had a baby at fifty plus! And what a husband! And me, says my mother, I thought what I thought: She finally had the baby she couldn't have, and I knew how. One doesn't really need to be pregnant in certain cases. That's the story: The biggest fruit was always in her dish. As if it dropped out of the tree into her dish, that's funny, Mrs. D. says says she—says my mother.

—Tell me the end of George, I say.—What do you want me to tell you? says my mother.

"George, littlegeorge"; I stretch out the hands of my voice. Bent over the little cot in Algiers parked in what was once the study of Doctor George Cixous my father, I hold out my voice, take my voice I urged him, I am trying to fish up the drift-child underneath the reflections of the silence the round face turned toward me lips slightly cleft I breathe the syllables toward his pointy tongue I want to inspire him, I want to lift him up to bring him back to the response. Without taking flight either he remains plunged in mysterious preparations.

Inhabitant of the tongue. So, as there is no one save the ghost of my father in the room where I plead, I catch hold of him, I draw him up to my breast humming a song I lick his gills and the dim nestling gives a shiver.

—Come on, George, says my brother, come little brother says my brother, up you go, onto my back, we're going for a ride, come little brother says my brother the hospital resident to my son the lamb nestling turned up out of the blue. With a flick of his wings there he is perched on my brother's shoulders. Whereupon my brother with his graft-brother on his neck tosses his mane, they trot along the corridor of the Clinic picking up speed, galloping, neighing, the little beak of the child-supplement cracks open at length. Then from the mouth twisted up in joy, ripped from the awkward stopper too big for such a little jar, spurts a cry of laughter, and a dew of malice spreads across the pale round of the face. At the gate to our childhood, head between the bars, I look on: the marriage of my brother the doctor with the misfit but not missing child George. We were always missing a third, I thought. A brother and a sister want a baby. We never stopped begging my mother for a third after the war. The war is over where is the baby, we demanded. What did you do with it, what are you doing with it we hounded her with our words. Where is my brother says the one where is my sister says the other. I raged. My brother shied. Brutal, out of breath with the hope that was waning, the child, the child! tomorrow! Tomorrow will be too late! We gnashed our teeth. We turned the house upside down. We were nosing out the hidden child, the egg, the fruit of our hostile embraces, a sister for me, a brother for him, the war flaring up again, you need to be three for each to be himself or herself, enough of this Siamese stuff, we wanted the third who unbalances and liberates. We lifted the rugs in the living room, tossed the cushions aside, opening the napkins, shaking them out, sniffing in the drawers, without being able to renounce finding what we were looking for.

It's Omi who spoke to me about it. Yes, there really is a ghost, we are right to feel it. But for my mother it had never existed.

And now, fifteen years and forever after we stopped waiting, it's my brother who had finally ferreted out the Easter egg as if during all those years when I had quietly renounced he had patiently continued excavating the house in Algiers, breaking into the sideboards, detecting the keys hidden in the piles of underwear and even in Omi's cake pans. He had found his brother. The dough hadn't risen properly, as was often the case with the *Gefüllt,* the work of Omi, the cake of cakes that we adored not like something to eat but like the household god, whose difficult preparation we followed with passion, all the more so as half the time and with no explanation—the measurements being always the same—the god refused to rise. He was a little flat, the skull, the back. But even so. He's short a little nose, a little of everything. But it is the child my brother in the end had never stopped dreaming of. The very one.

—It's my little brother, says my brother firm cold stiff with resentment. You leave him alone now, now I'm taking him.

The scene takes place beneath the silent gaze of the tribe of the dead. Me too I observe the scene. In this scene I am one of the dead. In the arena my brother rears up and neighs defiantly. Half-veiled by the cloud of dust a three-legged foal wriggles between the impatient legs of the elder brother.

I might have thought he was going to die, but it was impossible, I could have imagined it, hoped for it, but it never occurred to me, I feared for his life, a child that doesn't swallow, that doesn't take, that doesn't hold, that doesn't keep, that half drowns in the air just getting from one breath to the next but dying, it never occurred to me.

Just because he'd been born. He'd had the strength to no longer not be.

The tenuous, the improbable. And I am the one he happens to. It's a blow that upsets my life. A revolutionary event. We left in the opposite direction, my life and I, my thoughts, the scenario for the future. In the space of a month everything is replaced. Where there is City, there is desert. Where there are books there is the simple child, the nestled dimling. Where there is a long road stretching from side to side of lands and worlds, there is a corral. Inside it we live a bird life my six children and I nourished on berries and crumbs. There are no more slices of time. Not ever believing he was going to die. Because he was born. We have twenty-five years to live or thirty says the Pediatrics and Maternity Book.

—What beats everything is that in the days of George my husband you had to die. And now the opposite. But the most extraordinary is that each time the family takes one road, in the bend the road takes a turn in the opposite direction. You settle in for thirty years or so, you plant the oak and the pine, you carry up the stove, hoist Omi's dining room set which for fifty years has been following us from country to country. And the next day, you're off again. You should never settle in. *Man wird so alt wie ein Kuh, doch lernt man immer zu.* One grows old like a cow and still one has to learn and one adds to what one has learned. But it's not true, in the end, one grows old and one learns nothing. Me, I believe in chance. It's all chance, says my mother. The only thing you can count on is chance—on which one cannot count. This child, when did he go? *The only day* I leave the house. For one year I don't go out. *One day,* I go out. And he goes. Without me. *The day I am not there.*

—It's all a matter of luck, says my brother. Luck has always been good to me, except sometimes. I had this child. I used to have fun with him. Insofar as I was capable of having fun. As he could have fun. He looks, he smiles, he bursts out laughing. An abandoned child. With Mother for a mother. I was upset with you for having left him to Mother for a mother. But in another way I was happy. But if you hadn't left him, would I have found him? my brother wondered and me too.

—I didn't forsake the child thought my brother, each time my sister forsakes him I unforsake him, at first I'm mad at her afterward I'm happy I accuse her of crime against maternity. Then I am mother brother father and all parents. God keep me from ever marrying my sister from whom I am so different. Thought the storm my brother. And me I trembled under his stormy words. And I found the sun that had been denied. My brother piles up pyramids of heavy gray clouds to muffle the frail and tender as the flesh of a chicken liver heart that nestles in his shirt. It was pouring rain. The child safe in the vest pocket of the shirt, head propped on my brother's firm breast.

—You wouldn't have that child rains my stern brother, his eyes hard and clear, that's what I thought, he says.

It rains off and on, storm, brief clearing, shower, that's precisely what I thought he thought, I thought to myself, seeing him now with eyes barely brown now looking black with anger thinking in oscillations, thinking he had thought then having thought the contrary after having thought what now he no longer thinks he thinks but still a little overcast a little off to the side and threatening and using only the murky, disquieting past indefinite which could be an error of tense but which flooded his phrases with a painful timelessness.

He has a false image of me I was thinking, he's not fair to me, that's what I thought but, if I put myself in his chair, it's perhaps the way I would see things, our judgments are entirely false or half-unjust according to whether we sink up to our ears in the left armchair or the one opposite, I huddle in my chair thinking I find him unfair and off the track, each of us thinks: unfair wrong, and each of our exchanges is abruptly unfair and sizzling, the further we withdraw the harder we strike, we fling a stone over the armchair and drop back down behind it. One ceases to think what one thinks for all there is to think about is throwing the first stone and throwing again at the first possible chance.

—You *cast off* that child, my brother comes up with, you *cast off* that child because *he is monstrous,* says my brother. That's what I thought. Says my brother still thinking what he once thought and what today still I would hardly dare think. And yet. Beneath the rough words, I am shaken.

—I don't think it anymore, says my brother. But having ceased to think that thing in those words only recently, he wasn't yet used to thinking differently.

Crouching behind the chair at war I hear the screech of missiles, not aimed at me, but which want to strike the sister of a brother that my brother no longer is. The danger remains real. The more my present brother distances himself from my brother of yesterday the more the blows rain thick and fast and the words detached from the subject acquire a harshly poetic strength. The words of my brother are a little male, wherever there is a risk of tenderness, but that diminishes with the help of time, it's normal. Me with my brother I am a girl and no doubt about it.

George we call him the child. In truth it is *the child itself,* the cause of our passions. A childhood has us by the uterus of the heart, it grips the walls of the ventricle with its weak suction cups. One must not cast off the mongolian so long as he has not come unstuck by himself, otherwise part of the heart comes off with him and one risks leaving a bit of placenta in the uterus. It's what makes us bleed. Today we are going to check the condition of the heart.

It was sudden. The death. One day, says my mother. The outing. A Sunday. One never goes out. One Sunday one takes a little jaunt. It's inexplicable. And when I come back the Staff says: During your absence, the child ran a high temperature.

In this story Algiers is the navel of the world, for it is the seat of the tribunal, the family with its pure of heart gods and its unjust gods, its cast of the wise and the wily. In the center of the City, the Clinic opens, a synagogue founded by my father Doctor George Cixous, then destroyed, abandoned, deserted, then brought to life again in the hands of my mother the Midwife Eve Cixous, resurrected as *the Clinic* once more. The place where hundreds of newborns come to be admitted to life or to death each year. The cord is cut. The child is weighed, measured, looked at. Here the child is decided upon. Judged. Certain are well written. Certain are uncertain. The Clinic is the door of the world. The navel heals.

The Staff thinks. It's quite a blow. Is it a tragedy? It's like in a tragedy. That's for sure. The thing could only happen the one day of the year when the guardian is off duty. Right away the child runs a very high temperature.

Just that day: that very day. He's thirsty all the time: Sunday. The Staff says: He would drink up the sea.

—I let him drink drink drink says my mother, and she goes on. Still today. Drink drink drink. In secret, I drink. In the study. Every word. Still.

—There's nothing else I can tell you. I thought he was going to die. Such thirst.

I see she can tell me nothing more. I'm thirsty. I can't ask for more. I think the story is going to flicker out. *The badly written child*—that I wrote badly. And centuries later, trying to fish up what's left of it. The end, there it is, now, this year one year, nothing special, just suddenly this thirst. Terminated. My mother adjusts her earphones in her ears. She is still on France Culture. She is listening. I watch her listen. I'm thirsty. I say nothing. She has eyes only for her program. My thirst, my thirst. She says: Oh! indignantly. She adds: That's incredible. When it's finished—the program—she goes on.

—I thought he was going to die, says my mother (and she says nothing more than what she says) but I couldn't bear it. *Just the day I wasn't there.* The sentence alights, neutral, giving nothing more than what it gives.

To finish up this slender thread of a tale she says:

—One night, he didn't wake up again.

She adds: In the morning he was cold.

So, therefore he was dead. It's a modest end, unobtrusive.

That's the end of it. She sticks the earphones back in. These days she is never without her little portable radio that I brought her from the States. She listens to it. She doesn't listen to it. It's a total attachment. She's speaking to me. In the middle of the conversation she brings in what's on the radio, summarizing and transmitting it faithfully. There are always several of us. Sometimes she is accompanied by a little static. Night and day. At dawn she reports on what the night has told her. We are never completely alone. Sometimes I get tired of having to shout to make myself heard above the other voices. I don't want to live with the radio, I shout. I rip off the earphones and I shout even louder.

She has finished. Eyes turned toward the universe which speaks in her ears, she has returned to the present. Leaving me alone with this past which has nothing new to teach her.

The door to the Clinic falls shut again. I saw nothing.

—I still think—says my mother—I can't decide if she is talking to me or to the other.

—I thought however, speaks my mother—it was a solution—all the while the radio in her ear—I was very fond of him—says my mother. It was better he die—says my mother the level voice of my mother.

I listen, riveted to the words, wondering how to punctuate, if I should put a comma or a full stop or delete the dashes or the spaces, how to interpret her speech underwritten or broken up by the other one, the radio? I note, picking up the thread again: "I was very fond of him it was better he die it made no sense to want him to force himself to live which is what he had always done up to that day living out of a sense of duty to life, doing all he can in spite of his cardiac malformation. With a smile."

—I don't know if he's aware of the state he's in? Suddenly my mother raises her voice.

—Who? I shouted, who's not aware? Now we were talking awfully loud and then louder and louder, my mother shouting out of deafness from listening to the other, and me shouting even louder to try to reach her, without the least idea where she was, was it in Algiers, in the Clinic, or in one of those countries she's been traveling to lately with France Culture as if she were there, Russia maybe, where she was an hour ago. Even when I'm there, even when we're eating, she prefers the radio to me, I thought, the friend on whom she can depend. She doesn't hear me.

—She will continue later, says my mother. She takes the earphones off. And she continues:

—I don't know if he is aware of his state. Does he know he can't read or write? I don't think he has a big vocabulary to express anything. Is he aware he can't do anything without his mother's help? I only recall how he used to smile. Is he waiting for the one day I wasn't there, to start dying? Does he know it's better to die exactly two weeks before the birth of the next child, in order to disappear at the very moment one can't allow oneself to think only about the dead? I am a little dubious. I see you must think that, but that's one of your ideas. It was sudden just a day when I went out I come back and he's running a fever of forty degrees. He left as suddenly as he came. Unfortunately it was much better for everybody. It was the right moment, but was he aware?

My mother was shouting while we were talking about the child, though there wasn't any wind, but it's that she heard the ghost of a speech which however I was not making.

—You'll end up saying it's George, the cat! she shouted and I was caught unawares in my thoughts. That he chose the day, I don't believe that either.

I know how good and tactful he was. But that's my idea. Is the mongolian aware that one can choose? He is in the dark.

Then she slams the door of the shadows and coming back to the light that no voice haunts she says there is chicken for lunch.

—No chicken, I say.

—A scrumptious chicken says my mother. Free range. Lying, my mother, I know her ways.

—No, I say, no chicken, and I hear my voice precisely reproducing the voice of maternal stubbornness. Over chicken we scrap like cocks.

—No?

—No.

—I know you I know your foibles. Says my mother digging her claws into the living room sand. It's tooth and nail now. And just because you know me you know my foibles you cook chicken, I thought astonished my mother pigheaded.

—Bless Montaigne who could not bear to see a chicken slaughtered!

—I bet he ate it all the same my mother clucks.

She calls that weakness-for-chicken. Now we are cackling.

Chorus of Battery-Reared Chickens

O all of us the daily specials
We are the most neglected of all animals
Our number innumerable as the stars in the sky
And the sand in the sea
No one cares about us, no one takes pity
We're of no account in the world's philosophy
We are mothers stripped of our carcasses
No one can bear to look at us
No wonder no wonder no wonder
Mile after mile of wire cages we are crushed together
Behind the barbed wire we are jailbirds in stripes
This is the reality
No hope of one day being a free chick
No chicken ever able to extend her wing fully
We are antiquity's butt-end chickens
Chickens with wings for nothing, no sooner born than our goose is cooked
Our lot in life is to be turned on a spit

O we the most banished of all living creatures
We are full of sighs our sighs don't interest you
We are the death squad chickens.
One dead chicken, why should you care
Not even victims and not even executioners
We are born cooked
And yet
In each condemned chicken
Never having been a chicken by creation created
In each bird dead-on-its-feet
And who's to believe the raw thoughts of a chicken
One quick step from barbed wire to barbecue
One heart beats you and me
In every chicken weeps a chicken who knows
Knows nothing, never having known
Remember the days when chickens would peck in the yard
We have never lived but still we suffer
For never having had that which we never had to lose
Like free men do
No one can look at the miles of chickens
Without shuddering with a very old anguish
We are the crucified miles
No one wants to contemplate our calvary
Mile after mile of chicken to feast your eyes on
But you don't see them as you head for the table
What men do to one another's chicken who will broadcast the news?

—Chickens also think.

—Jews' chickens don't suffer. My mother lies and believes what she says.

—I ache for chickens, I say. My mother has better things to do than to listen to my Chorus; there's an exciting program on the Concentration Camps.

She has withdrawn into her program and she leaves me to my cackling.

There's no one like my mother for cutting you off and terminating things.

Whoever's had her on the phone has had it—clack. After the full stop no dash. Never any suspension points. Ejection. She cuts the cord. Not immediately. As long as the cord beats, as long as there is this communication between mother and child, as long as the cord *beats* one mustn't cut it.

When it stops beating you cut it off, one inch.

Now she's squawking. You are squawking, I say. Squawk? She looks up the foreign word in the dictionary and doesn't find it. So chickens don't even squawk anymore?

The breeder sticks his hands in the door of the cage and pulls out two chickens in each hand. He grips the four chickens like so many leeks. Heads down. He holds them by the shoulders of the wings. The chickens scream, because they are real. They make an effort to struggle. They have no illusions whatsoever. A second later the breeder crams the chickens into a hutch, beaks clipped. Destination: final. The breeder is not the least indisposed by the screams of the chicken. In this film one doesn't see the breeder's breeder. But there is surely one who plunges his hands into the human shadows and claps hold of the human chickens by the shoulders of their wings.

A chicken may die without ever once having had a chance to spread its wings created by God.

I've eaten. I've saved no one. Save one cat for one million abandoned. You can't not live, says my mother. Live abandon kill not look desert.

Flee, says my brother.

Where? How? One can flee everything, family, child. Sister brother mummy Omi me. It takes courage. I never had the courage to let go says my brother.

I shake off fleeing. The courage, I thought, is not in the courage to flee. It is in the courage to watch oneself flee. And the greatest courage of all? I never had it. How can I speak of it?

Overnight I ceased writing and I began a mongolian life. I abandoned the idea of City and the idea of scientific research, the idea of streets swarming with ordinary human beings, the idea of numbers and norms, I gave it all up. The idea of going from school to University and all those ideas of circles and societies, I let them all drop at once and I went off in the opposite direction, following the mongolian's instructions. I closed up shop, I canceled the fashion subscriptions and the political engagements and I headed for the forest. I entered a life I had never considered. In everything I followed the directions of my dim nestling. I attuned myself to abandon, I submitted to the boundless authority of boundless impotence. Overnight I converted to the extraordinary. Up to then, starting from the heights on the outskirts of Algiers I had always aimed for the center of the City and as City I naturally targeted the capital. Within twenty-four hours I turned on my heels — as soon as I'd skimmed the article "Mongolism" in the Pediatrics and Maternity text — and I followed destiny's arrows. Going instantaneously into the paddock marked beings otherwise human. About turn. Never again shall we come back to the Cities. Life pivots. First lesson. Reality is a theater. And me I'm a character who used to think she was a young woman. Suddenly I had met up with fatality. The world is a Greek summer and mocking. One walks believing oneself to be on a road. Wrong. The road gulfs. Cut. The gulf yawns. About face. Tragic irony came out of Shakespeare's plays and cast its sticky net over me. In the middle of my room, a trapdoor. Astonishment greater than horror. Everything needs to be reconsidered. Destiny has wars in store for us and they break out without being declared, mad, crazy, when there is neither sign nor reason. Oh now I understand all the words I thought were reserved for the tragic heroes, chance, destiny, events that don't lend themselves to laughter, mysterious designs of well-concealed authors, arrows that pierce your foot during the insignificance of a stroll, it's for the masses too, it's for me who am you, I who am knocked over by a black chariot drawn by wild horses on the steps of a rented house. You've been found. Wherever you may be, I was making coffee, I was peeling carrots I believe, or perhaps in the bathroom washing as usual my daughter's underpants. Omens? No omens. The twilight of a morning, wind rising in the branches of the oak, no thunderbolt. Drums? No. The garbage collectors. Nothing special. No foreboding. And that's when. Something happens, it's not nothing, it's decreed. The letter says: About face. And truly, here begins a life in the opposite direction, an entire life. All of a sudden everything I would never have done, I did. Up to now I'd planned to see the different continents. I called off my tour on the threshold of the expedition, I ceased to be a nomad, and I put up the mongolian house. Henceforth we too would live in the company of affectionate animals.

I prepared for the siege. We are attacked: The enemy is one of us, the enemy is the weakness and the fragility of the smallest among us, the peace of the most peaceful the enemy is in our arms on our laps, as soft as he is sharp.

I elaborated a plot from the inside out, I invented immunities touching our own offspring. We were going to live on three legs for one, for another I'll increase our population, in the herd one will no longer pick out the odd one. We would league ourselves together around him. To shield him from everything to shield us from him or vice versa. All my thoughts could be read in two ways closely connected by a resistance which never wished to declare itself. Even today I reject the word *hostility* it was much more complicated the hostility that united us was the antique obligation, the eager consent, the arm suddenly trembling that grips the uncertain child that slips a little too much not enough and within it runs our blood stumbling and stammering, what was right at home there was the submission to Designation the messenger in charge of handing out destinies whom in those days I didn't call God. I decided to increase our bodily numbers without losing a second, seeing to the size and balance of the herd, I shall dilute the rough-wooly lamb with no nose in a bath of brown lambs with healthy bleats and muscles. The more turbulent children there are the less the odd one will stick out. I foresaw the irradiation. Against the irresistible flash of mongolian we were going to line up an entire infantry. In the ensuing months I counterattacked with a pregnancy, not weakening my position by giving any thought to it. I made ready. I put up. We raise the walls of the house in order to close ranks around him. We adopt his description. It is a language, a tongue. We adapt to his jerks and jolts, she yaps, she hobbles, she has the same rustlings, same friction same brakes. We too we shall enjoy music. I undertook a methodical adoption. The skin of the mongolian, grainy warped awkward, I pull it on I slip the whole outfit on over my soul.

—He never had any teeth, I say.

—Just "before" says my mother he had two teeth.

Suddenly I am short two teeth. Gnawing at me suddenly inside my heart.

Overnight I converted, and I adopted *the famous mongolian line* the one I hadn't noticed at first, the sign of recognition concealed in the palm of your hand. It was an alignment but on the nonaligned. At twenty-two years of age I had just discovered the other world of the world, and in a single blow. Nobody had warned us. My mother either, the German midwife in Algiers nobody had told her about the other human beings even if up to then we, the family, we knew the other humans were the Jews, that is us, it was us, our family that on the one hand fell back and increased our numbers in order to resist our own strangeness, it was our own besieged house which ended up cracking its seams and overnight, my mother abandoned the direction of Berlin, and turning her back on the north, went in the opposite direction, according to the directions of the boundless impotence which when one points it in the opposite direction contains boundless power. That's how she arrived in the South and as far from the center and from the origins as she could make it, while by another route all the other members of the other family also went as far as possible from the most City of Cities to the most peripheral doors of the planet.

Now to our astonishment suddenly we were outflanked by a people of whom we knew nothing, and perhaps who knows a people even more ancient and most anciently banished and denied than ours but which at that point had no history. I was troubled, I felt a flaw in my philosophy, I entered a state of uncertainty especially about the definitions the limits the borders the barriers the species the genders the classifications, on the one hand hadn't I been born mongolian having given birth to a mongolian, and therefore born of his birth, but on the other hand I thought nature not being finite and defined but open, riddled by chance couldn't anything and everything happen to us and we be, god, animal, or immortality, by slipping through one of these unknown holes?

How to hide this nose newborn?

The mongolian crystallizes attention, says my brother the pediatrician.

To the supermarket the mongolian goes with his mother, for the housewife doing her shopping that day it's an extra. She buys the oil on special. And in addition she has seen a mongolian trailing his mother up and down the aisles.

One cannot keep him out of sight behind the fingers of one hand.

Fortunately says my brother there are no more of them. In four years at the hospital I haven't come across a single one. When I was in Israel says my mother I saw a whole troop of them they brought to the pool. They were good swimmers being very supple. For the thirteen-year-old girl traveling around England, the mongolian having his dinner is un-settling. During the meal one doesn't take one's eyes off him insofar as one cannot take one's eyes off him for the mongolian's siblings mutely and ferociously harry the visiting girl, with stern looks they fly over the scene dive-bomb and fly up again which doesn't keep the girl from be-ing attracted by the enormous uncoordinated vitality of the indefinable at table. The mongolian being is like an awkward marionette, he puts his hands flat on the plates he darts jagged looks across the table, he or-ders and disrupts the whole company, he provokes the curiosity that he forbids. This is where the visitor realizes her power. He who repels her attracts her in spite of herself in spite of him, she is jerked from sym-pathy to antipathy. Sitting above the table on an invisible balcony the fam-ily brings the weight of its mongolian law of silence to bear on the en-tire visit.

These days one detects them and nips them in the egg.

Soon there will never be any more of them says my brother. With a few exceptions.

Later we will not know what he brought to us in taking away what he gave us in deporting from us what he caused us, what damage, what muta-tion, what heartburn what emotion.

—Is he aware that he doesn't know how to write? wondered my mother.

To be aware, yet another question. And not just that: to be aware of not knowing. But are there not other sorts of knowledge and other types of consciousness and other sciences, the nestling inquired of me? How should I know?

The most precious thing in the world for me at this moment, the crea-ture that feltseemed like another me it's the cat: She doesn't sit on my lap, nor on my bed, nor on a pile of books, from among all those pleasant possibilities, she chooses, sitting right here on this page, to which she fits herself, in the place of the writing. We agree on the place.

In the place of the writing: *my son, the ghost in command of the writing.* The ghost writing of my son the mongolian. I gave him the place of the writing. The boundless whiteness, the unqualified, the unqualifiable.

I am still on his page. Still on his mysterious Culture. He is come. Not the messiah. The other messiah, the bizarre, the doubtful, the feeble, the provocateur, the sweet congenital. He does nothing and everything is thrown off balance.

But before him, an omen that I only deciphered in retrospect, there was Omi our grandmother. The wound, the beginning the first three-legged dog, the first crooked cat, it was Omi, who would never stay properly upright. She's the one, the smallest of the family who opened the door, she was forever tipping over, she loved Strauss waltzes and sunsets, and at the end of her interminable life, when she stayed on without the help of any illusion, the life upright no longer held any interest for her.

That's when we didn't kill her. But fortunately for her for us the child-grandmother didn't find out it had been abandoned in the meadow.

My mother is still with her radio, her little playmate. Or maybe the radio is her ideal cat, the always-there the purr that doesn't go away and leave her and especially pours into her an inexhaustible and never-ending supply of words. It's not that I wanted to give her a radio, it's that I understood she was asking me for the object on which one can always count. Give and shut up. The radio, Omi's last friend, last companion of those who can't keep up with the grown-ups.

Last night says my mother it was on gladiators. After that it was Derrida's Travels.

OMI, GEORGE, THEY NEVER STOPPED ATTACKING ME and me defending myself, should I complain? Because of their violent weakness I never stopped writing and not writing, rewriting and stopping writing but always in relation to the necessary writing, and it was always to resist their invasions and their storms.

The last time, I made a note of it. The dream of 1/9/98. We were in the small sitting room and Omi let in the following caravan: a little cart, a pregnant woman, an old lady, a slew of children, on the cart some bundles and a big dog, not to mention the rest of it. It was the dog that ticked me off a whole great German Shepherd. I rushed over: Out! There's a cat here. Omi had opened out of an ancient instinct. One sees a pregnant Moorish woman arrive, one opens, it's for the midwife. But that's all past history. It's been twenty years since the Clinic went out of business. In fact these people came to the gate seeking shelter. They told us their misfortunes. We gave them an hour to be gone. In such circumstances I take my notebooks and the cat. Or the cat and my notebooks. They had picked up and left, women children and a train of animals. And they were trying their luck in the neighborhood. Who kicked you out? asks my mother. The man. But, it's urgent: The dog, I say, out. Too bad. A dog as big and thick as a tree trunk. Tough, if he goes away, tough. I led it to the gate. On the way there was another dog gnawing on some large bones in the garden. Not without disgust I picked up the bones, ribs along with the head of a black sheep. And I lead the dogs out. The black sheep too. Out. Let them stay at the gate or not. But no way we're going to keep them in the house. I saw clusters of little naked children gamboling in the street. It was the Clos-Salambier. I went back in, dogged by a handful of kids. We'll have to bring all these people up. I give it some thought. Feed them, we could for a few days, great tablefuls of them. It's not the money. It's mainly the writing and the cat which are in danger. What am I going to do with all these three-legged people? Unruly boys. The prostrated woman. A baby perched on the hedge thickly tangled with roses. Things look very difficult. And all because Omi opened the gate by mistake. A small invasion, and it's treachery. So not only am I going to have to sacrifice everything that matters most to me to the first refugees who come knocking, but also there's the mob of all those whom I absolutely refuse to admit, that I don't want to hear about, and who are already starting to yell about injustice and distress, I am therefore forced to thicken my skin, I put the big dog out who is not hurting me but my cat doesn't want, my garden is chockablock with a flock of black sheep, I go by the condemned as if I had judged them, as the young doctor on the ward passes the bed of the boy crushed between the jaws of the rocky black sarcoma without so much as giving him a second look, one cannot look at those one does not save, one looks away, because the minute one has caught the eyes of the resigned, that's it, the door is ajar, one is attached. The fact is one cannot kill what one sees. One cannot see oneself, one cannot be seen, refusing. Had I gone to the gate instead of Omi I would first have inquired what those people wanted, I wouldn't have opened without asking. But I was upstairs in my hideout writing, and Omi didn't want to bother me. It happened. I'll not complain.

Omi has changed a lot. In the old days she was offensively rude, she stamped her foot in the kitchen to chase beggars away, she shouted in German, *solch ein Kukuck nochmal!* she brandished the ladle, maybe the broom, and slammed it down on the cat, dog, gaping snot-nosed children, zealous galvanized soldier, they were afraid of her, and fled the fires of her blue eyes who would have borne anything without batting an eyelash. Even the rats cleared off. Now the reverse, as if she had replaced herself, what she used to repulse she welcomes, charmed, disarmed, stamp her foot never, she opens the gate, she hands out the keys, she sets the broom down. I don't like this one bit.

—At your age, I cried out, you shouldn't do a thing without asking me! But what age? Having reached a certain stage on the road, one no longer knows, one goes farther, faster further beyond, it's elsewhere it's all the same.

I should have kept my mouth shut. Am I going to scold my grand-mother for her new tricks? New blunder, new patience, new lightness, new agility. In the old days she never made enough food to go around I used to think, it bothered me, now, it's too much, hardly has she finished prepar-ing some dish and she's off on another cake. Plus, she is growing smaller and smaller. Now she's as big as a ten-year-old girl. Where will it all end? In the old days she used to gut chickens that had been running around the chicken coop that morning, her hand without memory and without com-munication. What do Omi and the chicken have in common? Out of life and into the pot, presto, the soul is on the bed in the bedroom, it doesn't come down to the kitchen. And now docile getting itself plucked?

I would do better to follow my memories back to Algiers and from there to the Clos-Salembier. We came out of the house usually under attack, hand in hand to the municipal library one must cross the vacant lot en-closed with barbed wire, hand in hand, two are better than one, what Omi used to call: "we-two-girls" without our being able to decide who was pro-tecting whom, she and I the same twelve-year-old size, and the same desire stronger than our fear of receiving one day stones the next insults. I'd do better not to forget our endangered childhood.

THE MONGOLIAN THERE IS THE TRAP: The strongest child is the weak-est therefore the strongest, the mongolian doesn't see the danger, one takes one's eyes off him, he's dead, a child who totters, one must watch over him constantly, not only does one live from one moment to the next but in ad-dition one catches oneself making a dozen mistakes a day, it's too much innocence in the house, as soon as I see a person I love start to resemble him I am on edge, I bristle, someone who grows old without being mean, alert, uh-oh watch out, this niceness I know it, this smile which has nothing hiding behind it, this total lack of ruse: the supreme ruse. The moment I see on a familiar face, my mother's in particular, this slight vagueness, a line missing, especially a lack of attention, especially this being off guard, this offhand manner she's had several times recently of giving me the slip, like that morning in February, visiting the shore of a lake in Eastern Tunisia and all at once I see her doubled up in the yellowish water, I shout, I jump up and down, she's OK, fine, I set her up on her feet again, she says she wanted to grab some things on the bottom, but don't you see this water is totally polluted, littered with trash you'll catch some deadly disease plus she is drenched dirty hair slicked to her head, a joke of a head, teeth all crooked, one thumb shorter than the other, as if she were mimicking the little clown, as if the original model of the clown had been a mongolian, forever topsy-turvy, forgetful about death because he has such love for life.

I've noticed that in our family the women become mongolian again as they grow old, it's what makes them so charming, it's what bothers me: Every summer I feel as if I can see my mother slide a little further into that excessive niceness, for sure she is nicer and nicer, and some days she remains in this oblique state a little off to the side of the state of waking until almost ten o'clock in the morning, the eyes she drifts across me a little hooded.

I bristle. "Anything but that!" as she would say. There I am hair on end, back arched, ready to pounce, I spit, I snarl, I even screech, even cry in a raucous voice "Mother! Get back here!" I scold her. I cling to her: "Stay here!" I order, and I jab my finger toward the ground. She's drowning under my very eyes again! She hurries up, and paradoxically starts to slow down, that's what it is, full speed ahead, she's picking up speed slowing down, I know exactly where that road leads and who it's imitating, that speed too, that lack of coordination I can't bear it. Were I to go along with it, that's it, she would be accepted in this new state, she would be forced upon me like that, and I would treat her with the consideration due a wizened infant, I would finally have agreed to let her cross to the other side, then bye-bye, she would be my shrunken grandmother, my hobbledy toddler, in any case I wouldn't worry about her anymore the battle being done, lostwon, I wouldn't be there rattling her bones and bullying her whipping her up with orders, bellowing into her ears which she has a perverse tendency to plug, to keep her from going over to the slowpokes, but perhaps

I thwart her wishes I insist she prefer me when perhaps her only desire is to stop being a sensible grown-up person, she wants to gabble, talk gibberish, otherwise why does she have this haggard dim-witted nestling look until ten in the morning this slow-motion half-baked look, that's not her at all, I am irritated, I've been through that already, I am frantic or else she is deaf but if that's the case let her say it! But at ten o'clock in the morning, the veil lifts, her eyes take on a familiar roundness, good-bye the dread the mongolian steals off into my limbo, and it's Eve! my mother in person, she runs to the market.

This mongolian future that pounced on us all I had to do was read the Newsletter of the White Butterflies, the Association for parents of mongolian children, and we knew the future. I was only twenty-two when the mongolian Revolution broke out. For parents the mongolian is Professor of upheavals.

With the mongolian initially everything is by chance and then on the contrary everything is foreseeable.

True-mongolians says my mother they have just here the nape completely flat it runs into the neck.

Why he has this Chinese look, I do not understand says my mother, this Chinese look therefore not Jewish but not goy either. It's my grandson she says, and from the shelf of her mind she takes the wink-eyed child. It takes some getting used to, the innocence of this innate wink, the way he watches us from under the sign of irony, with the gentleness of one who doesn't know evil from good. He can swim says my mother retarded but very sturdy. Except George who doubtless wasn't going to swim because of his heart which didn't close properly. This very affectionate child loves to be caressed. Finally the mongolian is nothing surprising once you get over the big surprise. I donned the mental outfit of the White Butterflies. I became a parent member of the Association. I write the Association. Why butterfly and why white I am greatly curious. The answer doesn't arrive. Something remains blank. The rest we know. Save the exact date of death but the mongolian death will come to George as to his fellows, of the white butterfly family, earlier than the average death of the human being. The mongolian being matures otherwise very slowly very fast toward death. Death is a white butterfly in the heads of the parents. Association of Butterflies. In the distance, society. The Association of non-Butterflies.

I had just bought myself the *Encyclopaedia Britannica* I'd ordered the *Larousse du XIXe Siècle* on credit. I had written the first chapter of my doctoral thesis when overnight I was transferred for a duplicitous chromosome

I'd never heard of, I was recovering from having butterflies and it wasn't a metaphor. The separation took place in the wink of an eye. My whole mongolian life I spent it without any compromise with my previous life, separated from the woman I had been, who was forever out of reach. I had given up writing, another species of butterfly. Change of country but on the spot. Besides hadn't I been warned by a book? I recall having rejected Ecclesiastes just the previous spring when I'd come across him on the garden path. The minute I read him I called him mad, criminal, king too, or head of state. With him around, I sleep with one eye open, the chief in the mask of a grinning demon. Everything he says is all very well and good but I clearly saw the two serpents dozing on the ground, the very big one and the smaller one, their bodies like steel gray thin viscous worms, on one side the sun on the other such melancholy, a man bitter tired discouraging. Nothing but leafing through him I guessed: There are two possibilities; either the chief provokes a massacre and the world ends, or seeing that we are prepared to counterattack he crawls back into his shell and that's the end of it. I used to tell myself, my son arrives (I was six months pregnant) he'll be a good ally. Already I was on my guard. One time I grabbed a not very big stick and I brought it down as hard as I could on the little snake. Unfortunately without killing it. The beast ties itself in knots, divides, escapes I even try to trample it, no luck. The chief watches me flailing around with an ironic air. When my son is born, I thought, I will take up the fight again, we'll deal with the big snake. Now I saw Ecclesiastes bending his mask over the cradle where my dim nestling my ally is snuffling away. That he has not yet killed Ecclesiastes for me is perhaps the sign he believes I've trespassed? Or he has renounced his monstrous project?

The Clinic

—"The Clinic" says my mother, all of us say the Clinic as if we were saying: the Port. At other times it's: the Temple. The Castle. The Divine
Comedy. The Great Gate and in the middle the river, my mother poling
the boat and one moment Hell the next Paradise. The only Clinic in Algiers where there weren't any cockroaches, for the good reason says my
mother that-e-ver-y-time-a-room-emp-tied I fumigated with a German
product. It's a small box, you set it on a brick, you light it you close everything up tight. And the cockroaches were an-ni-hil-ated. Whereas everywhere else in the whole City it crawled with them. You close the door and
that's it. A German product, naturally. This product disappeared afterward. After it was forbidden. I don't know why. It killed all the pests.

In the old days in the time of my father it was a hymn of praise road we
took from the hydrangeas and the palm trees by the house barefoot dawn
lively cool crisp at the shoulder a downhill road from ecstasy to ecstasy toward Belcourt cutting through the Little Wood which rendered us sacred
underfoot the red earth and pine needles, where the sentinels (what my father called the human excrements) in the shapes of cakes sprinkled with
flies stood drying at the edge of the thickets and which, after an hour during which we grew increasingly loving and attached to one another, my
brother and I, set us down in front of: the Museum. It hardly mattered
what was in it. It was the noble destination.

Now all roads led to the Clinic. The slosh of buckets the footsteps of the
women in labor in the corridor the cries the calls for help the efforts to rise

above the condition of being a woman in this City, all the women who climbed slowly sighing as they went, features drawn anxious wondering how God would provide for them would they be spared or executed. Once on the mountain the struggle began. One kept on to the very end. The Clinic of the very end, the denouement. What the woman needed to be saved was a child and best of all a son. A son who answers to the husband for the woman. The husbands few and far between, out of sight, feared. The child a duty a copy, a debt. The child for the husband. All these children who are bits of the husband, given back to the husband, these owed children, the chips you counted on to save your skin. Only the little mongolian is free of charge. On one side all those newborns heavily laden, all those offspring who entered into the family calculations, those children made to save their mothers from opprobrium, wrinkled trophies the woman counts on to obtain indulgence or her life. On the other the free of charge, the mongolian.

Right away the Staff gets attached to the freeloader. A real and truly child, neither promise nor threat, upon which the whole world can exercise its right to love. Chip withdrawn from the game.

—Poor Zohra says my mother, such a good cook. A woman cast out. She had to work for the wife of her husband who had repudiated her because she doesn't have a child. He was a motorcycle police officer and when he was in jail the other cops put her to work in his place. She spends an hour feeding him carrots after work. Then there was Miss Sharpshooter a bigmouth whose grandfather had been in the Algerian infantry, says my mother, a real brute, one day I see her shouting at a woman in labor: "Shut up filthy race!" "But, I say, it's your race!" One day I find her in my office. And what do I see? Who is dandling the little mascot? I didn't recognize her. A horrible woman and there she is laughing and joking with George, *even Miss Sharpshooter he attached her.* Not asking for anything except: love me. Not: help me. The word just next door: love one another's race, the other same race.

At the Clinic one goes in in order to come out with a child like in a child mill. One goes in with a tummy one comes out with a child, one goes to the exam, to the wicket, to the jury, to customs to the police station to the tribunal, one passes or one fails, guilty, ejected. A feeling of barrier floats in front of the door. The main thing is the exit with child. Some enter without their safety belly, the belly dangerously inhabited, some with a big reassuring belly, some with a flabby belly as if in imitation of big, some their belly disgusted, fed up, filled once more it's the tenth, in the corridor the two rows of anguish meet, the first-time anguish and the multiparous anguish and the two anguishes opposed but what these women come in search of mostly in the child mill, it's the certified child, especially the first at all cost. Afterward if God wants one thing and its contrary it's the accumulation, and the decline of the woman and the family in consequence of more and more children right away the necessary becomes catastrophic, the children keep coming, one is forced to want them, one cannot escape them, so the woman has to blame God for it or whoever created this infernal treadmill where you are forced to do what shortly becomes the ruin and misery of the whole family as if one conformed from birth to the mysterious decree of misfortune, all these people who are desperately dependent now upon the child which absolutely must be obtained, the certifiable, now upon the child who turns up with a vengeance, a calamity, with always one more child hovering over the family heads in an unbearable imminence. Her whole life the woman spends it in this persecution now running after the chip now fleeing and always only winning in order to sink more deeply in debt. But the most anxious of all is always the one who hasn't yet passed her childbirth certificate. And on this anxiety are edified the castles of State, Social Security, City Hall, and to round off these innumerable plots, an essential character in the comedy of Algiers: the Chief of Police.

The Clinic was the only maternity home founded on the famous German traits cleanliness, organization, hygiene, discipline, incorruptibility. In all the other Clinics, where there are cockroaches, there are also all the customs and manners of non-German nonmythical midwives. For women on the one hand the Clinic is a haven of health, on the other they don't find everything they could hope for: all the things that cannot be mentioned or avowed or shown and which are the subchapters in the epic, the shy tricks the stratagems and desperate disguises without which there would be no theater and no literature. Here one enters Science and its goddaughter my mother.

—Me I never had a dead woman, says my mother. But at the others there's a little of everything. The women are in danger on both sides. One, the husband waiting in the corridor. Two, the midwife who takes a toll on the victim at every stage of the trip. On the one hand there are the false midwives, the self-proclaimed midwives who have undertaken invisible studies the midwives with their diploma put-away-safe in a bank vault in France so that nobody in the world can ever steal it, there is the midwife trained in the waiting room of a doctor, the midwife trained as a cook another is a nurse's aid, all midwives who fear nothing, stillborn children that doesn't frighten them; then there are the midwives who having been trained in the hospital and certified with a diploma not-put-away-safe are nonethe-less afraid of everything, they are never absolutely sure if a woman is preg-nant for real or for a joke, then you have the group of false true midwives who don't check and take you at your word, if a woman claims to be pregnant-on-her-word, she is pregnant-on-her-word, if she gave birth at home on her word not having had time to get to the maternity home, the delivery having broken every record for rapidity, she has given birth on her word. And the child? The child? Unfortunately it didn't have time to live. Dead on delivery. And the body? The body? It is buried, where? in Baïnem, where you bury them. The child dead on your word. Everything has existed disappeared on your word. Except the birth certificate. The certificate is the law and it's cash. The various emotions secretly at work during these scenes would require a delicate and complex analysis. Each person is divided into several persons some good the others bad. Each ghost has its secret that it will never have a chance to confide to a soul trained for regret and misfortune. The forest of Baïnem exhales in the wind and in vain tales destined to abortion. A popu-lation of ghosts in the branches of the pines. Nobody listens, there are so many of them, the laments share the fate of the sentinels, we go by without seeing them the tenuous and sand-choked heroes, refuse of furtive destinies, naked feet protected by an antique indifference.

In the Clinic there are no hiding places and no mixed feelings, divided into opposites. It is all bright and clean, floors scrubbed and no cockroaches.

The building superintendent has no cadaver to chew over. It torments him. A famished cockroach.

Algiers is a school for actors and modest great actresses all the more con-vincing in that if one doesn't believe them something dreadful will happen to them.

Who then is this impressive group of women who come forward beneath their veils like game birds beneath the storm clouds of Algiers, to which mis-fortune relate them to which anxiety? The hunt doesn't lack for danger. If only there were a directory of doors at which to knock good for fending off ill luck! Blood, blood, the theme of blood marks their lives coming not com-ing sign of success, of failure, indomitable prophet, enemy and guardian of women whose dreams and their interpretations it regularly betrays.

In this country one makes blood lie. One makes it rise up again. One makes it speak, pretend, go in the opposite direction, fall silent.

This is the story of a person at the end of her tether whose three sisters gave birth in the Clinic says my mother. All big women all married to truck drivers. One of the sisters the biggest says mother a strapping big woman and she doesn't have a child. Until the day she was pregnant but every month she bled. Thanks to the incompetence of a doctor and a midwife. The huge woman. The midwife writes her a pregnancy certificate. For the bleeding the doctor prescribes her a preventive treatment. So she doesn't lose the child-at-last. In this condition she comes to me one day with the certificates. So you are pregnant I say says my mother. No says the woman, says my mother. I'm here to give birth with this girl who is pregnant. Being unmarried she doesn't want to keep the child. I'm taking it. I am paying for the delivery, says the corpulent woman. It was thanks to the trucker, the husband being absent or the delivery wouldn't have gone off so easily, which wasn't his says my mother. And thanks to those two incompetents she has the pregnancy certificates. You make me the birth certificate I'll pay says the fat woman. The answer to that is no says my mother. No to that, you haven't given birth says my mother. Not wanting to act in this play. The delivery yes the paper no. For the woman it's a dead end. The girl about to give birth. The corpulent woman. The competent midwife. The truck driver's wife at the end of her tether. What to do? So says my mother at bay I have a friend who is less of a stickler than me, I use these words, *friend, stickler,* says my mother. Go and see her, I say. You say you didn't make it in time, says my mother. She writes the play but she doesn't sign it, thought I. This midwife being a false real one says my mother she is not going to look into whether the mother has any milk or not, that she hasn't got any blood. She will write the certificate as if.

—But still today I don't know if I too am guilty, guilty of what? I say, I don't know says my mother, I'm trying to figure it out, says my mother, one opens the door of the Clinic and in comes a catastrophe that takes you hostage in a story you mustn't ever repeat, I say to the truck driver's wife go to my friend who's not a stickler and don't tell her the truth which she could have told her but what's the point, the false real one not being a stickler, so the truck driver's wife acts out her comedy and the midwife acts out her comedy, both of them act out their comedy to one another, there is no witness, therefore there is no proof, while at my place at the Clinic she tells the truth the woman, how to do otherwise and look where that gets us, the whole world was now at bay, already we thought we heard the noise of the truck returning, and how would it end, in the absence of certitude, we were nonetheless fearful, for a business which for nine months had luck on its side. During the whole pregnancy by corpulence everything went smoothly, whereupon she comes to the Clinic to the competent midwife for the delivery. Where is the justice? I ask you. For the false pregnancy the false midwife, but for the delivery the real one. With me there wouldn't have been any real pregnancy only an apparent pregnancy. There I could sympathize. Guilty of having sent her off to the other maternity home says my mother irritably.

If I didn't feel guilty says my mother I'd feel guilty. And look what happens to us at the Clinic because of these impressive women whose fear of the truck driver gave them extraordinary courage. When the child was born she wanted a boy obviously it was a girl. Too bad. To top it off the child of courage and of fear has a totally malformed ear. She has no ear I say to the mother, that is my mother to the big woman. Whereupon the doctor says it's a bad sign she may also have internal disorders.

Too bad says the wife of the truck driver, *it's done-it's done,* I can't go back, and that's all I know of this story says my mother.

Those are secrets says my mother which remain secret even to ourselves still today, secrets born of the Clinic, of courage and of fear, of the struggle to respond to the blows of fate, secrets stashed away in the hold of the Clinic, where it sank like a stone in the middle of the City of Algiers. I shouldn't have told you says my mother. But I should have felt guilty with regard to the Clinic if I didn't tell what I shouldn't tell. I've already forgotten dozens of stories, and no longer anyone to remember all those women struggling in that unique place the Clinic abandoned forever.

Too bad if I am guilty *it's done-it's done.*

One must imagine the four big sisters, the children the four truck drivers, of whom one and one are without children, the baking hot roads, the stops in the shade, the anguish and relief of the fourth truck driver one must imagine the pregnant girl of whom the story knows nothing, one must imagine what the woman thinks unstoppable on her secret road, she plunges on, the truck of the four sisters, a tire bursts, too bad no reverse, it's not a boy, it's not a girl, nonetheless it's a child, in flesh and blood. In the office she has a look at the nonetheless-child my mother's. A somewhat Asian-looking boy. He was already a little too big for the truck driver's return. Too bad says the chorus of impressive women.

— Guilty of what? I say.
— That's what I keep asking myself says my mother. Guilty of having given her the tip. To go and see a dishonest person, says my mother.

And now she feels guilty for having said this word *dishonest*. Because up to now she'd said "not a stickler."

—I had a hand in it. Me I wouldn't have made a false certificate. She hoped that I was going to make her a false certificate, some hope. But I never faked any one, she concludes uncertain.

But perhaps she said: But I never failed anyone.

Guilty of having failed someone guilty of never faking one, guilty of such purity that she feels guilty, therefore is, of being without fault.

—You've got to imagine the hustle and bustle, so many women enter and leave, they spend three days they stake their lives on it, leave and in the space of three days not one of them is recognizable, they all look alike, already you can't tell them apart, they come in big soaked in cold sweat mute or the opposite, they go out quick less big or more it all depends and all a little plodding, some lighter on their feet a sign of luck, others dragging their feet the verdict a little overwhelming, I see so many women parading past, you see them in bed it's one thing, you see them up it's not the same, me I make them come back the following week, it won't cost them anything but at least I can check what state "she" is in, even if I don't always know, not being a physiognomist who "she" is, my mother says.

If I am guilty I am unaware of it. In my opinion we are all innocent together. But there's a judgment that wants to bore a hole in our hearts to let its worm in.

All those women accused of child, of no-child, of child not like this not like that, all those guilty by definition, who come to plead their case, their condemnation, getting their tongues and feet tied in knots, committing faults and proofs to the world in the hope of getting around their punishment all those heavily laden who file through the waiting room where my mother now shuts her eyes now opens them and all of us secreting ruses and silences unceasingly weaving modest little webs in order to try to camouflage the evidence of the crimes they haven't committed, O piece of paper, I too know it, the fateful paper, stamped, the visa for a stay of execution, for a provisional acquittal to be renewed.

In the Clinic my son grew heavy with meaning.

All the patients who come to give birth and take refuge and spend three to five days during which time they're on the lookout for an idea, that's all the time they get in the infirmary, that is in private with themselves before returning "home" where nine people live in one room. As soon as they enter with the baby the idea of an idea goes out. After all giving birth has always been the occasion to give birth to a parcel of one's self. Dream and keep it to yourself. For a woman the Clinic is not without some secret advantages. For two or three days she feels free. Everything she'd had to do to bear she felt she was doing it on her own initiative this birth for two or three days was the accomplishment of her own will, for a few days this baby is her idea.

—For the births says my mother the entire Staff turned up, it was a fiesta. For the delivery there was the cook the cleaning woman the mother a sister or two. The Chorus cheers the woman on. The cook forgets about the kitchen. The Staff pushes. Push, push. The Staff laughs. It says funny things. The woman hasn't time to feel any pain. The Staff laughs. She pushes as well. She laughs. It pushes. There was a woman says my mother, in fact she was a Jew, says my mother authorizing herself to use the word *Jew* which she fiercely forbids me to say. For my mother claims one must never use the word *Jew* in front of foreigners. Which foreigners I say. You, says my mother, you talk to foreigners says my mother. To get back to the delivery room where there's always nothing but women, this woman was saying: Me I always pass out after delivery. And me I was saying says my mother, here, at the Clinic you don't pass out. So when it's the delivery the Staff arrives to laugh and joke, there's Zohra the cook, Barta the cleaning woman, Maria the hunchback, and the woman doesn't pass out.

This story was taking place in the continuous for every time the woman was coming back, she was not passing out. This was: the Staff's triumph.

—To conclude all these stories you mustn't tell anyone says my mother, they are secrets. She proclaims this to the company at large as one says in French another of the expressions she picked up when she arrived in Algeria. Her first move always having been to pick up the most outlandish expressions, while I at the beach I was always picking up the bits of mother-of-pearl and today still which are the glossiest most polished till they sparkle like the sea's fool's gold expressions.

Pearly secrets they are, whose exact value one doesn't know, it all depends, but all carriers of a germ of death or maybe prison.

Afterward I tell the secrets but in secret, I don't tell my mother about it, what I do is her secrets I keep them secret for her but not for the time of times. Hence in disobeying her orders I obey her most secret wish. Why otherwise would she confide to me with such care all the secrets with the warning "do not publish" unless to draw my attention to her most hidden her most perilous treasures. She verifies that I have got it all down, she asks me over and over again if she has told me the story of the big fat woman, I assure her that it's done-it's done, she doesn't believe a word of it with a great fuss she starts up again, and at each telling adds as a premium an infinitesimal detail. It's a secret, it is what she leaves me. She tells me don't repeat it. I catch the inflection. That means do it and don't tell me. Put me to death but don't tell me you are doing it. Betray me betray my secrets. Everything I am telling you is to betray. I have confided. Now take up your sword and brandish it. *Deine Lanze* that is what she calls my pen.

Having lost the Clinic with all its goods and hands on 31 January 1971 is still a source of pain for her. The great ship went down in the space of twenty-four hours she had just time to jump on an Air France flight for Madrid with the suitcase, the one and only, the crazy mad suitcase, the bag of secrets, the one fugitives take, the idiotic, the secret sharer which contains on the one hand the dregs of the remains, the not-to-be-relinquished debris, on the other hand the voluminous and totally innumerable and indescribable ghost of everything one has cast off lost given up to the nothingness which occupies the space of a life. The suitcase-portrait and résumé. The generic Suitcase all those who have panicked and jumped ship know its force and its absurdity. It goes with her, no, she goes with it, the last object, the miserable link it is all our worldly goods and all our shame. The Suitcase takes all.

That suitcase! a mirror one would like to smash, one clings to it O last cradle carry-on coffin.

—With one suitcase and not two beside me I had only one suitcase in the house an old piece of luggage the most banged up naturally into which I put only the most essential items says my mother, toiletries a nightgown naturally a dress. Otherwise everything precious quickly we pack it in a large cardboard box which never turns up, the bedside rugs the blankets the carpets the Algerian things, the belongings from the country you leave never turn up, each time one flees leaving a big cardboard box behind, which is how the family is supposed to have left a big box in Dresden, a big box in Budapest a big box in Osnabrück and now it is the Algiers tumulus, none of them turn up, you dream of them right to the very end. Thereupon a thin layer of earth, coarse grass covers the infinitesimal pyramid, seen from above one clearly distinguishes the shape of an eagle with outspread wings, here in this street a tribe has toiled.

All that's left is the decrepit suitcase The Mess itself a survivor from Hitler's day it follows us like a fate, empty and full, the old hand-in-hand, the hand one takes wrinkled rough, and a little moldy. Something ancient and dumb in its dog-eared look keeps us from discarding it. Probably it will follow the family exiles for another fifty or a hundred years and until extinction, lame old she-dog relegated to the cupboard under the stairs. It's like the fabric from George's crib a Moses basket my mother lined with blue-and-white gingham. The cloth is still around. Today cut into little sliding curtains over the vents in the cellar. No one sees them. Gay absurdity cutting across centuries, fossil vestige no one dreams of touching. A weak charm sees to its maintenance. Infinitesimal veils of shipwreckedness. Moth-eaten castaway of drowned time.

Overnight the Clinic goes down and on 1 February 1971 not a trace remains, therefore not only the ship the City of Troy containing how many other ships of Cities similarly swallowed up on the heels of the fugitive among which the City of Berlin, the City of Dresden, the City of Osnabrück and suddenly my mother loses the Clinic whose walls had once upon a time been bought by my father. The total obliteration of the birthplace of tens of hundreds of babies. But what took place in the book of the Clinic, the episodes beat out to the rhythm of blood and sobs, the gifts and jokes of the gods the shudders and prayers of the players and the playthings? Could one conceive of a salvage operation? But not my mother, recuperate those frail remains, only *One* is capable of doing it, my mother is unable to want to retain, the courage and the fear are missing, and besides it's her law, to depart in the company of the old very old Mess, sole witness of her panic-stricken retreats.

And no compensation, ever. To lose everything is the condition of her unsinkable competence. All these stories must disappear it's her wish. All these stories must be saved without her knowledge, it's her desire. You're not going to tell about that, the German midwife advises me in her sober voice. Immediately I make a note of it. One must recount only what one must not recount. It's all interpretation, translation of a tone of voice. I obey the order that she does not wish to have given me. One must be meticulous. In the margin I note each inflection. The essential is in the intonation. According to the color, happiness, misfortune.

I put the tape recorder on the table. It is very small. Right away she got started wait wait I cry out I haven't pushed the Rec button yet. Now, I say, and right away she begins again, careful, a Pro of spontaneity. A genius. Undamaged. No indemnities: The end never catches up with her.

"So what do you think, what do you want to think, what do you think you think, that I am going to do with all these secrets?" There's a question I never ask her, and she neither doesn't ask it of me.

Give me what I am unable to want to want give and don't tell, give me the secret of the incalculable adventures of the secret.

Does she know what a tape recorder is? Not really yes or no. The machine didn't work. We are not surprised.

WHICH DAY I DON'T REMEMBER DID I SEE HIM AGAIN once twice thrice in Algiers and it's always the same his/her smile him at seven months me at five months, me at seven months plotting the understudy two-timing him with the child to come, each time I brood on the way he doesn't become the way he stays as if drowsing there in the cradle a pinch of the eternal each day more defined.

An urgent curiosity stirs within me another astonishment rouses me, what became of him in the meantime, this life he led and which he led me for so long and always with the tact of one who emits a secret radiance and takes himself for nothing, a dog half-buried in yellow eternities, a sublime minuscule dog with straw hair yellow nose lifted toward the saffron yellow sky of the world, a dog whose docile profile is half-sunk in the infinite sand, a cradle dog slowly fought over by life and death, an indelible ochre puppy between an infinity of forgetfulness and an infinity of memory. Now he's coming back up, it's the hour he resurfaces, why now, I ask of him.

What are my friends going to say, my eternal friend, what will he say, to whom I never spoke of my son the transgressive the first? Will they believe I hid him away, dissimulated, kept for myself in a drawer, lost, denied like a god, forsworn like a faith, made up for a book? Have I photos of him? Any old photo of a mongolian will do.

The reason for which I have never mentioned him is so diverse there's a bench. But I'm not alone, we all kept him quiet and without a word and without breaking the seal affixed decades ago. It couldn't go on. Now the book was also becoming involved. Now it wasn't just us, family, memories and amnesias, there was a book which had come along to add itself to the confusion, if I wanted to sleep it woke me up, the book never sleeps.

The Burial

—The burial, I say pushing the word slowly toward my brother.

—*The burial?* says my brother. He takes the word and tosses it back in my direction. The! bur! yal! that's how he chops up the word, he dismembers it, as if he were biting into it. Back comes the word in pieces, as if I had tricked him by sending him a clump of earth in the course of one of our battles in the Clos-Salembier, that word he hurls it back at me, that's how I realize I'd thrown him theburial harder than I meant to.

The-burial-I-never-thought-about-it, that's how he catches my question.

But the battle already began an hour ago, it broke out between us without warning, it's childhood forever flaring up again: When I bent over my brother's big body deep in a roll of siesta a while ago, wanting to draw him from sleep with a sister's gentleness, I grazed his ill-shaven left cheek with a kiss. That's when he'd opened his eyes grown enormous with haggardness, and without seeing me eyes wide with a dread dreadful for me he had let out a terrible cry: Aah! What have I done to you? Whether he roared that or not I heard the groan of a man who is mortally wounded.

Just in back of the sleep one must believe there had been a blow, wound, attack, murder perhaps between us, without my knowing which of us, which weapon, which story—the antiquity of which blow? —Was it perhaps the kiss—that I'd given him? I should not have touched him in his sleep. But when should I touch him if not while he sleeps? So he starts up betrayed and he brings his horror down on me. I don't even know why I kissed him.

Maybe because he was sleeping? Perhaps because at that moment I was thinking of my son the dead of whom I hadn't stopped thinking for several months now, to whom I hadn't given a thought in thirty years my dead son so seldom embraced. I had a kiss on my lips, it slipped.

In truth there is a kind of folly in this kiss for we never touch in the family it's a tradition, there's no reason to cut the thread with the lip scissors says my mother and in principle we avoid infringing on our neighbors. As a greeting, we bend briefly to one side, we show a leaning. It's already very strong.

Knowing how explosive we are it's a precaution. That's why so often we are laconic, especially my brother, especially my mother, we measure out our phrases carefully, one spark and a fire breaks out.

The kiss slipped all by itself. And in the end it caught my brother the biggest the strongest the most warrior of the family. Everything about his way of leaping up and his fright shows I took him as a traitor and in spite of me.

But this whole story has fallen back in the past. Now we were up to our chests in the deceitful chairs. One thinks one's going to sit but the bottom drops out and one finds oneself half-buried in the chair scrunched up under its arms, muzzle lifted toward the yellow ceiling, and that's when I get going on the burial. Half-emerged, with nothing to lean against, deprived of dexterity by the perverse squish of the seat. Which takes all the spring out of the discussion.

—I don't know where he is buried, says my brother. No. No burial. No burial.

Burial of the burial?

With little gestures hindered by the chair arms he brushes the idea away, he casts off the little sheet of earth. The little face he uncovers is gray. But my brother drags his creature out of the tomb.

Bury his baby? He has sat down on the ground beside the crib with its bars and he's weeping. All the necessary tears, all the tears for which the child had such a thirst, he let them come. The child drank his brother's (my brother's) tears, he who could never drink a drop of milk.

—I wept. I was moved.

And me half-swallowed up by the armchair I also drink them these tears. And I don't say: Thank you, it doesn't know how to be said, thank you for what you have given because you don't know what you do, because you didn't spill your tears as a libation, because you were wounded, because all of a sudden they'd cut your leg off and you were hobbling, thank you for having nourished the dead, I didn't say it. I drank in secret. I am careful not to offend my brother with praise. Between us everything is unsaid: love with hate, hate with love. Secretly my brother is good, in hiding from himself. Not gentle natured. Severe: good. Good but not kindly.

The Clinic is abuzz. Three babies are being born. The Staff thinks: This fever is not going down. It's taking a long time.

—He must have been buried says my brother but not by me. I was very attached to the kid. I don't ever desert him.

During the battle we pitch lumps of sun-baked earth at one another, we shelter under the ramparts of the upturned wooden armchairs, we formulate death wishes, the clumps are so dry that they burst with the shock and return to dust.

What I feared most of all was the sharp-pointed iron bar that my brother was brandishing. Fleeing I prayed to the gods: Don't let our wishes be granted.

It has been many years since the wars ended. But the fear remains.

Nesting Boxes

It wasn't a burial, says my mother. She is stringing beans. She doesn't talk with empty hands. Children got put in the cemetery in *cubbyholes*. There was a wall filled with pigeonholes for all the little children. One puts them in *a box*. And the box in *a niche* which is closed and that's it.

I try to imagine the box but it slips away from me.

One took him to the Jewish cemetery,

Who was *One*? I wondered. Was it my mother?

I think about *One*. It is a pronoun which could designate either my mother, or my mother and my brother, or a person who went to the Jewish cemetery instead of my mother and of whom she speaks without naming her and who is perhaps when it comes down to it none other than my mother but afflicted, but lost, but distraught, but a little suppressed by the painfulness of the scene.

I think my mother did not go to my father's burial, none of us buried George Cixous, it's a thing we don't do, bury one of us no, the dearly beloved buries himself modestly. Later we get together in his memory on a slab of stone erected in his name. These beans were picked fresh this morning. Practically alive still. However in Algiers "it wasn't a burial" of which my son who was then my mother's son, was the object, or the character or the cause or the victim or the toy. In this case it is possible that One was indeed my mother. But the reference is lost.

My mother concentrates on the beans. With her left hand she catches hold of five or six of them. In her right the knife with which she snips off their little heads quickly and efficiently. It is not One, it is really she who is doing the beans. The beans on her lap. All of it vividly colored emits the infinitesimal radiance of the present.

—I have totally wiped out the conclusion says my mother concentrating.

—How did One go to the Jewish cemetery, I ask gently.

—One must have taken a taxi.

I imagine that One must have carried him. George. One doesn't know these things. During such moments One is elsewhere. One thinks about all the births. And on the other side all the deaths. Between which the taxi advances. My mother can't put the child in a box. She is attached to him. He for his part is attached to her. So One does it. One does everything my mother was incapable of doing: One puts the box in a niche.

My mother has no idea of the whereabouts of the niche which is in the wall where one stores little children.

Five by five, not a bean escapes. The Jewish cemetery is nested in the Saint-Eugene Cemetery like a box in a niche in a wall riddled with babies. I think of the names: George, Eugene, One. All these words which secretly become persons who change the words into flesh, in name and in shadow. Useless to think about the box. I turn it over and over: the Box: in every direction. Finally I turn back to my mother.

—There was a wall she begins again with sorts of compartments for the children. Which closed like safety-deposit boxes. Safes filled with peters and georges. Nothings. Or full of thoughts, or sentences, feelings perhaps, under lock and key, the wishes of the dead then? Hints and clues?

The box? A box in which one puts the dead person, of wood perhaps, who carried it it isn't me perhaps that's something I don't recall. In our family, says my mother, fitting a reminiscence into the vacant cubbyhole, with her way of never letting a space go to waste, one is incapable of attending a funeral. One is invited, one goes to call on the people, but most of the time one never quite manages to make it to the cemetery. Even if at the end of the day one turns up at the deceased's house, one no longer recalls who it is that is dead, the last time I went to yourfather's cousin's for her burial, the week before I was thinking of going to see her and I had so many things on my mind, I forgot, but when I finally got there the following week, for her burial, there was a crowd and especially lots of *candidates*. All those people waiting their turn. So just as the cortege is getting underway I notice I've left everything in the cousin's bedroom: my backpack, with all my belongings. Either I race back, but then I'm going to miss the departure of the cortege. But I can't leave my bag with all my personal belongings in this house the dead cousin no longer inhabits. How will I find them again? I wonder. The cortege. They gave me so many directions I never got there. Nothing interests me less than cemeteries when one thinks about it. Starting with Saint-Eugene where we shall never again set foot.

While I, I am disturbing fresh graves, what am I doing here stirring this up, I don't know what I'm looking for digging up the native land beneath my own pages, but I see that what I'm ferreting around in it's the native land, the one to which we are tied or denied, and at times tears rise out of the earth and condense in my throat, when I speak my words are wet. Perhaps that's what I want without knowing it, to weep? the Book in me asks.

—Look at her, all of a sudden, asking the family for something, something she's discovered she's missing, and what is it? A box? After all these years?

I can conceive that this is disagreeable, as if I came to reclaim a jewel which I had renounced in their favor or had lost interest in, there is no reason for them to give it back to me, they are not accountable, it's like stealing, taking back, and what next?

She wants us to give her George's death.

I myself do not understand me.

"Deceased in Algiers" perhaps but not dead at all not yet, no. It takes time. Things don't happen on the days they occur, neither the events, nor the people. My son didn't happen to me when he first arrived neither he to me nor I to him, he happened to me but later, already later. The day I wasn't there.

A little while ago, when my brother went, he left a great mark on the room and over the whole garden. I closed the gate that he always leaves open and I began to be buffeted by his great vertical gusts of wind, whose roots, when I examine them with the Book, are of an admirable depth: It's that my brother hasn't stopped blowing since the early days of his life.

I wanted to tell him—for the kiss—for the tears—I didn't dare—

But the things which have happened reach me so late, it takes them forty years to find me out and for me to find them, they take place long before the Book opens me. Then for the first time I enter the antique event. I am a being slow to read.

The Place that can only be the City of Algiers, says the Book. What makes Life like a play it's the importance of the Place. And the two most potent places, finally, are the place of birth and the place of death. Yet at his death, the human being is not present and yet wherever one dies, it is truly there that the life makes sense. Something warns us. One goes off to die in Berlin, one to Rome, one to London. Precisely. If my son George died and disappeared in Algiers it is not by chance.

Everything has happened as if someone had written this story in order for me to read it one day I tell myself. Nothing can separate me more from Algeria than our two deaths George my father George my son keep lost re-united gone astray on the deserted stage of Saint-Eugene. Nothing can attach me more to the country than these two dead.

To send the child to Algiers that I had left for good five years earlier it was to send him to the past, if I didn't think that my brother thought it, we used to think in opposite directions and everything can be thought in opposite directions, you refused that child because he is monstrous says my brother the pediatrician. The parents frequently reacting very violently. The mother kills herself the father hits the doctor the child inspires to each his own madness.

We were all very tense. A circus wagon at night: One hears snarling scraping scratching one doesn't know what closed-in thing still one is a little afraid despite the likelihood of bars. My mother always facing the crack of an exit, me clinging to the door without knowing on which side, my son glued to my hip like a dead leaf, my brother who sometimes rises standing like a stone above the pit sometimes rolls like a rock straight into a chair. Downstage, indefatigable, the nervous Book, wants, wants, wants.

The Fading

My mother having taken the beans and gone off without a glance as if she had received an urgent call, I was left in the kitchen with her sentences. I listened to them again. Simple sentences but the more I listened the more they darkened, gathering clouds, detaching themselves from my mother and rising to the ceiling. "What-do-you-want-me-to-tell-you," that one for example I'd let it pass without paying attention, now it came back new, invented, abrupt, even it addressed itself to me in a sharp tone of voice, authoritarian, it struck my ear all of a sudden with a trenchant little flip of its wing, the room was traversed in all directions by flights of veering sentences, I suddenly caught sight of a black tail, a white belly, a flash, I saw that I had seen nothing, I had kept to the gray areas, a mist without angles and the orange note of my mother's cap to lure me away. Always this anachrony called *Treppenwitz.* She had said and I believed I had heard. I thought I began to hear something in between. She had said to me "what do you want me to tell you?" I had taken those words as words for nothing, words of a dozy grandmother. Yes what had I *wanted* her to tell me, I asked myself, had I wanted, had I asked her to tell me what, what did I want that she mightn't have told me. Concerning events turned to dust. There was therefore some object to want. On her way out my mother had darted one of her nonlooks at me from under her cap, a way she has of abruptly turning her back on you. I didn't let go. I don't know what I didn't let go of. But having once ventured so far in the direction of the abandoned places there's no turning back. Some expectation gripped me, a thirst but for no precise revelation. I wanted. I resumed:

In sum what my mother had said to me it's that he was dead of dying. He was dead of himself, of having been himself, and twice she had added it was better that he should not live. I thought it was better. Later on he is unhappy he is more and more attaching the family is more and more unhappy, knowing that he has no future, 50 percent dead before the age of five and the rest haven't got long, it's the king of the castle wrong way up and everything you think at the same time you think the contrary. It's good and it's not good. What is good is not good. Before-the-age-of-five it's when five years it's when is it one knows it's before. Before long. And "long" what's that like? And against my breast refused by the mongolian whose tongue is too cumbersome for the size of his palate, I clasp a clown who does not make me want to laugh. But just before having thought it was better one thought the contrary. At every instant, the contrary. What is strongest, it's the attachment, all the more strong as it is woven in order to resist a painful detachment.

Later on trembling with emotion one applauds at the sight of the mongolian running. The mongolian race is the remonstrance of happiness. Bobbing from side to side, hoppety-hip, one runs too and his face like a sun-ripened fig rosy and cracking from the inside out. One clings to him, it's shameful to hold on to the child who can't hold himself up in the wind, but not hold to him it's a betrayal, but if one could choose? But on the other hand, a choice was made, this woman was chosen for mongolian among all the seven hundred to a thousand other women. In point of fact the life of the mongolian is nothing but choice and betrayal that is reversal and passion. When one has a mongolian life to bear one has a mongolian life to revel in, in the long run one has a tendency to become more intelligent not to say better, it's a matter of keeping in shape, one must be constantly leaping from this side to that, or jumping over a rope or straddling a wall, and not simply looking at the garden but ceaselessly sweeping it with your eyes all the while doing something else, writing with one eye reading with one ear, peeling vegetables with one hand, and with the other, eye, ear, hand, one looks out for the mongolian.

All it took was for me to go out once says my mother. Here I am says destiny, it's Sunday says the event. And there was no final moment. Instead of a final scene there was a fading away. There had been night. There was night in the story. Sunday, fever, night. Place: the Clinic, nighttime. A night replaces and erases the final hour. The fading was beginning there, one no longer sees anything, one no longer gives anything to drink, and "in the morning he was cold" but this is a cold and lifeless remark to which my mother did not lend her presence, there was no one in this night, I tried to push open the door of this night but the door itself was a night while as in a dream I myself lingered interminably before this night which stole off and multiplied. Little by little but without degrees I made myself night I had no ending anymore I was dark night undifferentiated and all the while I was thinking this facelessness, neither humid nor dry without depth in which I am who knows if this is not the interior of his death a black dry water without thickness but in which all the same I was stagnating as I had seen my mother floating without breathing under a yellow water out of which I had dragged her but soiled but in extremis. But all this was improbable but moving.

Then the fading spread to all that came after, to the morning, to the break of day, to the discovery or to the establishment of the fact, to the sentence "he is dead," nothing of all that, the fading escapes us, it is nothing, a silence but lost and even the missing word weighs too much. The family did not express itself, the Staff thought nothing, itself faded out, not a sign of life anywhere,

as if the child had been withdrawn along with the story under cover of night

and the fading had next swallowed up the taxi, the cemetery, there was a deserted and unfathomable breach closed mouth of the story. And finally this memory of the niche but which contained no one, which was a skeleton of memory which one couldn't say went back to my mother—aside from the word *niche* which for me is sparkling—but for her a word like any other and the recital a recemetery.

And so there was no one

As if the word had got around, but which one

My brother neither

As if a word had been (given) taken back

As if-death-

The fading—I was slowly realizing—being itself part of the faders and the faded—the fading had had such force that it had struck all the people of the Clinic, starting with the eve of death, definitively *totally* my mother had said.

"I've totally wiped it out." I had taken each of her phrases for one of her emphatic German-style clichés. The extreme impoverishment of her story, I thought I recognized it, just what you'd expect, I thought, her frugal way, her absentness, her passionate refusal of any passion.

Gradually I perceived a strangeness, a similar fading, I had just come out in an immense amphitheater, no matter how many steps I climbed a very high wooden partition separated me from the person I was speaking to, only a partition, so that I heard her voice respond if briefly, but her, I didn't see her, we talked by flinging words over the partition, I raised my head during this cut-off exchange and I contemplated the incredible cupola of the celestial cathedral, an immense piece of work which gave me the splendid dimensions of our pettiness.

It wasn't in the least an impoverished tale, it was a stolen-away tale, a stealthy tale, a nontale, yes a refusal of a tale.

An ancient deed. Decades old. And me why did I come now before nightfall, coming back where I'd never been? Yes why all of a sudden did I come knocking. My mother was fleeing. Suddenly I sensed her flight. She is fleeing me. Like a doe, like a dove. Suddenly I heard the crackle of twigs, leaves. It is me she is fleeing. It wasn't at all what I'd thought—falling back on my own cliché, thinking of my mother's sobriety, the elusion her renowned way of bearing down on the questions, banging the phone down on the last syllable, of letting you drop. Not at all.

It was a vigilant wily refusing mistrustful tale. The more I play it back the more I am aware of the dry neutral sullen note, of a kind of fleeingness, of being put off.

All of a sudden I saw her darting sideways glances out from under the beans, all of a sudden I saw all those beans crisscrossing and multiplying, meanwhile my mother's orange cap was angled very low over her face, I saw her lips ever so slightly check the flow which she adjusted, feigning naturalness with a newly acquired skill.

And the more I play back the story the more conscious I am of a nuance of reprobation which had escaped me, a subtle anger or reticence, but in the background, dissimulated, covered by the vivacity of her fingers in the sink and in the end it's perhaps this infinitesimal excessiveness with regard to the beans that had attracted my attention, for all at once I noticed that I myself was enthralled by the quick march of the beans as if by a virtuoso demonstration. The language of the beans suddenly, suddenly I thought I saw its coded message.

What are you doing here? On our territory? Our memory was in peace. Scat!

As if I had exercised an undeniable right to curiosity because I was the mother and undue because I was not the mother. At this moment, the mother the whole mother it was my mother, and the night which was putting up its high wooden partition was notifying me where in all fairness my rights stopped.

Before me, but at a magical distance, that distance without apparent depth which is itself the essence of the impassable, my mother, pure defense, fending off, forbidding. I saw her clearly and yet she was hidden from me.

I tell myself she is refusing me the thing I have not deserved. I tell myself she is accusing me and forbidding herself to accuse me. I recognized the anteroom of the apocalypse. I saw the veil in which she draped the stubbornness of her silence clearly, it's a faded gauze on which one can still make out the trace now almost completely faded of what used to be blue-and-white checked gingham. All right, I'll go, I say. I take my coat. Suddenly the light went out. A sad yellow daylight seeped through the kitchen windows. And at that moment a clap of thunder shook the city — of an almost unbelievable breadth and duration — the trucks of heaven I thought. The noise rolled swelled up occupied every inch of the air. Then out of the noise came an airplane. Was it a plane this noise had preceded by several years? The plane appeared — tiny in the middle of a conflagration of boiling light, a sheet of yellow fire unrolling along all the streets and up to the summit of the world. Bombarded say I: a Butterfly — but the word was pulverized as it came out of my lips. The City Radio had spoken, the Voice raced through the streets — distant — I rewrite — chopped — covered up — swallowed — this is a rehearsal . . . of the truth . . . a rehearsal . . . of the truth. The simulacrum covered everything. You can't keep your head. I was carried away in the rumble the screech of the plane, a Butterfly. It had come. The thing.

What I now no longer wished to hear it tell me.

I have just understood I was thinking.

I thought: I have just understood.

I could have told myself: I have just understood!

But because of the presence of the book which is awake even when it dozes off, even when it allows itself to forget, instead of: I understood! right away I summoned myself back to the punctilious reality of the reality: No, I had not just understood, that sensation of light was nothing but one of my numerous thoughts, intense, contradictory, and I could have thought and believed the contrary. All this going on in my head as in a book. And it's the vigilance of the Book forever in the background which never stopped plaguing me with fresh doubt.

My legs were about to buckle. Oh if I could have thrown myself at my mother's feet. Tell her: I know.

She made herself keep me at arm's length I thought, to keep me at the distance at which I had lived for thirty years, she didn't allow herself to kick me, to chase me away, not out of tender love but as a mother's ruse so as not even to draw my attention. And now the veil I took for my luminous understanding was ripping. Now I understood that I had never understood. Now a dark red sun was rising. It was pouring rain. But that didn't help anything. Except the book.

A little later in the day I found myself in Algiers in a garden of lush green grass it was a big rectangular carpet. I recognized the dream cemetery where I have never been. In this vegetable patch, at the bottom of the picture on the right stood a tall piece of furniture with little cubbies in dark wood. I looked it over. The cubbyholes had names. I understood that they corresponded to presences in the garden. Suddenly my glance fell on the last little cubbyhole right down at the bottom on which I saw inscribed the letter G and next to the G in white letters the word *Tomb*. I bent down. I saw two little buttons next to the letters. I pressed, a spring clicked and behind the word *Tomb* a little cavity appeared. Inside a tiny chest about the size of my hand. Inside the chest a minuscule clump of earth. Furtively I took the fragment of my dead son. I broke off a fingernail-sized crumb which I wrapped in a handkerchief. My robbery accomplished I put the rest back in the little chest and closed it up. I looked innocent. I buried the crumb of my dead son in the bottom of my pocket. What hadn't been given me, I had taken.

Now seated on the stump of a tree, I spoke to him. "I wasn't with you," I murmured, I needed to hear my voice through the choking sensation that filled my chest, "I wasn't with you the last day but you, you didn't desert me," clutching my sticky thigh my hip palms without palmar lines glued to my skirt.

I'd always thought that my mother having had two possibilities when she arrived in Algiers with the child, one to kill it, the other to adopt it, had resolutely chosen the second (adopt). Had resolutely set aside the first (kill). After having examined them.

Now she had never heard of these possibilities.

I understood that I could have invented this idea of my mother's. As for her she reinvented the memories as time and events went by. Only the dates and the addresses resisted the multiplication of our stories. Only the incertitude and only the confusion remained constant. Where was I the day I wasn't there? And now.

She Is Upset with Me

What I started to think the next morning:—She is upset with me. She believes I don't know she is heroic.

But I can't tell her I know.

Those are secrets. Totally off bounds. What she's never said about the death of George and the death of Omi, or rather what she has always dissimulated about one death by the other, or rather about the life in the death. Secrets sworn to nobody other than herself. It's her treasure. It's her regret. It's the hidden gift that she has absolutely not given. It's her hour of greatness, hour of dolor, hour without mother without daughter without sister. She believes that I am unaware of her hour.

But I guessed. It was almost nothing, a way of not glancing up at one moment, a brusque acceleration before slamming on the brakes at the wheel of a sentence the word *totally* heard at a frequency which cannot solely be attributed to her Germanity, a few small grammatical slips, not counting the fits of sneezing not counting the outbursts caused by misunderstandings, aimed in my direction at the dinner table, not even counting the omissions and oversights, not counting the mongolians which seem to be popping up all over town this week like snails after rain whenever she goes to the market, signs that abound like ants, all excessively small which is to her credit, especially for the language, I don't even mention speech and tone of voice. But were I to tell her I knew I would remove the grandeur from her heroism. For her heroism consists precisely in never having breathed a word, in never having confided anything, to anyone, in having renounced all heroism.

She tells me: Pious Jews get insomnia. They don't know if they should spread their beards on the sheet or under the sheet. Sometimes she has insomnia. In this case she listens to France Culture.

It is a long and pitiless discretion. Each time I approach one bed or the other, she pushes me off irritably.

She accuses me of always having left her alone at the moment of her hidden glory. She is not wrong. We always left her alone. But on the other hand we always obeyed her law. She thinks that we should have disobeyed her but without telling. In this way we should have obeyed her unavowable wish.

But we have always docilely exactly let her be heroic. Left her alone. Obeying if not her desire at least the law of her destiny.

According to my brother my mother doesn't know she is heroic. Your mother doesn't know he says. She acts strongly without heroism. It is a dangerous kind of heroism.

I believe my mother believes that I don't hear what she doesn't say.

But who knows? There can be error. There can be truth. Who to tell what I think this morning? I tell the cat. I've nothing to hide from it. The cat is the mongolian who causes no suffering. This cat is perfect.

The mongolian does not hide. The mongolian doesn't know how to hide from us the imperfection he gives us to share. But we can't blame him for this. He is an imperfect cat.

My mother has gone out with my aunt. It is Sunday. This is an absolutely exceptional occurrence. It is not without care and precaution that she has left me at home, and not without assuring herself that everything necessary for my survival in her absence is on hand. I watch her go round the kitchen, the dining room, each room, she leaves me written instructions on bits of paper. She'll be back this evening at eight-thirty. She comes into my study one last time, takes a look around. Then they leave, the two sisters, in the German language. I do not tell her that I hear her bringing motherhood to incandescence.

The book urges me to return to Algiers. One more time. To turn up Algiers, to take a shovel to dig up the scene of the secret. For months now I have struggled to unravel this fading, I skirt the night, I'm forever climbing back up Isly Street now Ben Mehidi Larbi I haunt the memories, a bizarre pursuit, I finger the web I search for a hole, in my pocket I have the crumb of my son, the resistance of this lump is extraordinary. I don't even know what I ask of myself, if I keep returning to the scene it's that there's a smell a hair, I want to rid myself of a suffocating silence a silence suffocating my silence I stride on, the cloak of a lie over my shoulders, a short doe-colored leather cloak a lack of truth, legs naked up to the thighs, top muffled up, a shrivel of truth, I want to see my eyes I want to touch my hand, I grope at Algiers, I sniff I slip. I have to get back in mongolian touch, his death I don't want to give it up, I feel hunger embrace a void of truth, I *limp* it's that leg that's throwing me off, the cut leg.

Since I've been back I have had only to deal with impossible doors. My mother gave me the heavy iron keys of the Clinic, which was number 26 on the street, but among the facades this number no longer exists, I go back and forth a dozen times, finally between two big houses I think I can make out the trace of a 2 here and perhaps a 6 there. The facade of the Clinic is reduced today it is less than fifty centimeters wide. I approach with the keys they turn, it is well and truly here that we used to be, the narrow iron door yields and there I am where? In front of me as if through a peephole is a corridor the diameter of a water pipe carved in a waxy granular matter which lets through enough wan light for me to see to the back of this den which was once the children's house. You have to wriggle in flat on your belly. To the right to the left you can imagine orifices by which to penetrate shrunken rooms. The horror and the regret which grip me are huge up to the intense sky. Terrified I back out. It is the first time I am in contact with the cadaveresque reduction of a house. The Clinic is nothing but a mummy's gut. The Staff long since crumbled to dust. I hardly dare set foot on him, on her. Limp.

It is a mistake to knock at a dead door.

I go away. I have the keys in my hand, which do not die. I'm going to give them back. I've had enough. But the book doesn't see things like that.

The burial, a child in a wall one doesn't remember, a fiction, a death of dying an invention it's all her imagination.

One cannot stop in a hole without edges.

—THE FACT IS I NEVER ASKED my brother the doctor what my son died of, the fact is that until these past few days it never crossed my mind that my brother must have been at the Clinic in those days, when he was studying medicine at the Algiers Hospital, who other than my brother should I have asked, he was perhaps absent just that mortal Sunday, exceptionally, but it may be that he was on the contrary present just because my mother was out, I was turning this abstention in which I had kept myself for so long this way and that, I noted the components of this reticence with stupefaction, I could have thought of it and I hadn't thought of it, I noted my brother's equal and symmetrical reticence, he could have spoken to me and he had kept still behind his pediatrician's desk as if we had signed a pact which however we had not formulated. I was impatient now as if propelled by an urgency proportional to my interminable sleep, impatient to break this admirable spell. I rushed to my brother's. I burst into his office. I exaggerated, he thought, as usual. But I wasn't exaggerating, I was exaggerated, dragged, pushed. In the lunch-hour silence of the office, the noise of the other: He was snoring. I've always been impressed by the sound of snoring. It is god who sleeps, god the all—removed from our tragic excitation, the thunder god indifferent to worms.

—She doesn't remember the cause? my brother wakes.

—She doesn't remember at all either that or she doesn't remember that she doesn't remember.

—He had a murmur. He had an atrioventricular canal says my brother, and I follow on his heels as he races ahead in the medical foreign language. *Atrioventricular.* The long and musical and pure of any sense whatsoever creature spirits me off to a painless region. The-a-trio. A medical marvel. It's a world I discover, of which my son was the inhabitant. He had a canal, something unknown to me. I follow my brother's broad voice. We are in a lay chapel but otherwise religious. The priest's words have the beauty of something one believes in. Peace steals over us. I listen to my paternal brother and I believe. Which doesn't mean I see. On the contrary. I see nothing: I hear: I believe. Things that are somber and full of anguish become long, all-powerful names, which I do not understand. Submissive dominant peace peace for she who is gone away as for our neighbor, here is the story destroyed restored. The ventrauricular trio.

—He was a victim of congestive heart failure my brother spun in words above my head then he came back down in front of me. His heart stopped working. He was having trouble breathing.

Me I tried to see what I was hearing, I felt as if I was no longer very far from my son's cradle.

—He was a little gray, says my fraternal brother and there I hear well what he is pouring out for me to see, the wings of his nostrils which were beating, and I feel that he is giving me the child to understand, my dying son to touch, I bend over, and my brother also. He straightens up again.

—It's funny Mother doesn't remember.

My brothers straightens up quickly—me I knew how to treat the emergency. You have to administer digitalis he says very fast and diuretics make the child pee to reduce the volume of blood and you bolster the strength of the heart I tell Mother in a rush. Says my imminent brother. That's the way to stop death and hold on to life for a moment shouts my brother running to the pharmacy of the Clinic, where my mother always has what you need, he crosses the corridor in a bound tossing me the explanations. Next, hastily, you must operate but it's very difficult, it's an operation that does not often succeed running you grab a syringe I grabbed a syringe of cedilanide and Mother stopped me saying you have to let him die to my astonishment she stopped me saying let him die saying let George go she stopped me in my race with death, it was a very close fight and Mother stopped me choosing her side she told me let him go, right away your reaction is to help, the wings of his nostrils are beating you rush to help him do you believe right away right away your reaction is to flee, you're racing against death, but what does it mean to help in an emergency you are heading in a tragic direction but which you haven't time to think about and when there's no emergency you don't think about it, you can only really think about such things at the last moment, when the emergency lights you up and at that moment in the glare which would be propitious to reflection precisely you don't have time at the absolutely unpredictable moment when suddenly his heart failed you race to the pharmacy *knowing*, knowing that you have to give digitalis because that's what you learned at the hospital it's automatic, give the digitalis a chance me I knew what the treatment was at that point Mother put a halt to the knowledge, it's funny she doesn't remember, and he is dead.

—And he is dead, concludes my brother gasping out the news, to sum up and conclude and close the window, being naturally prone to help. And death finally and with tremendous simplicity entered our lives and our family, which at that moment could be compared to a dog with three legs. There was my son my mother my brother and I wasn't there. I heard him calling in the imaginary meadow: I am nice nice nice. I took George's body in my arms, and I said speak to my fatidic brother.

One cannot imagine the fragment of life which has flowed past between the moment my mother stopped my brother and the moment he died. One is unable to imagine the face of my brother and the face of my mother in the meantime. One is unable to imagine the syringe, one is unable to imagine the hand of my brother setting the syringe full of cedilanide down. These moments take place safely out of sight of the human imagination, above speech and beyond silence, at an infinite distance from all knowing. My brother speaks forty years down the line. On my lap I hold the transparent remains of George and we observe that time hasn't any thickness, or duration, or length, it has only an immaterial number, 40.

—I was amazed by yourmother's presence of mind for she was very attached to him, my brother comes back.

His way of switching from Mother to yourmother, this is the only sign of the change of epoch. We go into the corridor of the Clinic. And she was right. In a few hours he was dead. I thought it was a strong action. I accepted it. In a few hours she was right. It was a mental act, and forceful. The force was that it was a mental act. To stop the gesture and especially to stop me, it was an act which took place beyond the norms.

Had she *thought about it ahead of time*? I wonder, wonders my brother, but I sense that he doesn't want the answer, for forty years he has avoided asking the question it's a question one wants to shield from the light he thinks, but in the other armchair I am thinking that no doubt my mother can always thinkofeverything in her brief distracted naive swimming with the current life, but never would she have "planned-ahead." All the same, says my brother, the child was condemned in any case. The atrioventricular canal remains a very serious cardiopathy. What his future was that Sunday I didn't consider one doesn't reason one flies. The child is there one can't tell oneself he is going to die even if he is condemned in any case on the one hand one says he is condemned in any case on the other hand one does not pronounce the word *die,* if one said that to oneself ahead of time he would be dead in advance already one would arrest him in one's mind, you can't do that, he was dying I raced to stop his death whereupon Mother stopped me, and all three of us we stopped battling the current together.

In the big armchairs it's time for tea.

—She's a strong woman says my brother. It is summer. We are barefoot.

For me the strongest is that she didn't say it. Never. Forty years she manages to conceal her strength. Quite the contrary in my brother's opinion.

—She didn't say tell you because she didn't even realize it says my brother, you think? I say, realize what? I say, it wouldn't surprise me says he, the extent to which she doesn't realize has always astonished me, she didn't realize that it was a strong action, for me yes for her no, for her it was not even a strong action says he, that's precisely her strength say I, and afterward she doesn't even remember and yet he was astonished, for my mother never stopped surpassing our thoughts, without even knowing it and for that very reason, because she doesn't realize it, it wasn't an action, it was her way of following life's thread, right to the very end.

But I remember the string beans. The title of the scene would be: "betrayed in the nick of time by a handful of beans snapped too fast."

She darts a glance at me from under her cap: "You write you write everything that trots through your head." I am always with you and you are not always with *me in my hour of need* thinks my mother.

She's right says my brother and me I say, she's not wrong. And the book says: All that is written down. And it comes back to me Omi's phrase when she still had her wits about her: "Give me something and don't tell me," she said, my mother would say. And I didn't give her and I didn't tell her and I blame myself for that. But this phrase, isn't it also my phrase? Didn't I say that but not in so many words? I didn't even tell her give me and hearing what I did not say she gave me and didn't tell.

She doesn't know that I know that she gave me and didn't take it back. "Thought I" says the book. "Add those words" says the book. "She knows perhaps, and you you know nothing" says the book. I add: "Thought I." I admit it is prudent. I admit that I let myself believe whatever suits me. I recognize that I'd rather believe myself than believe my brother. And yet I recognize that from the point of view of a non-me, the book for instance, this natural penchant for myself does not guarantee the airtightness of the testimony. Me I would have stopped this quest on the page, with the sentence "she gave me and didn't tell." To end in secret would have pleased me.

But hardly did I close the door than the book opens it up again. The authority of a book is unimaginable: It is a judge.

—But why keep harping on these trifles? My mother is dismayed. "I've received a summons," shall I tell her that, no, obeying the orders of a book, I don't dare tell her.

But it's the last time! says my mother. I'm old. These stories are old.

So she says: *Your brother wasn't there.* Here is the truth: It was a Sunday when I was out. I'd left the child alone with the Staff. When I came back he had that high fever I found it strange just the day I go out he catches his death and of course if he has a raging fever like that the heart can't keep up. I was fond of the child but keep him from going no I wouldn't have attempted this is not a child who must be cured at any cost that wouldn't have made any sense at all to force him right away I understood that Destiny had knocked. I go out: Destiny enters.

And if your brother had suggested I oppose Destiny I certainly wouldn't have encouraged him to resuscitate him in the state he was in that's all we needed but he wasn't there not only was he mongolian already but to top it off suffering the sequels of such an illness after a meningitis I did not see what good could come of it, I certainly wouldn't have encouraged a child like that to survive if Destiny comes along and hands him a fatal illness one accepts and yourbrother was not there.

I was attached but attachment's not reason enough loving him isn't a reason to encourage him to survive totally absent and askew but on the contrary because later it wouldn't have been any fun.

I regret I was never heroic not struggling against Destiny, that's opportunism it is not heroism.

While my mother testified nothing but the truth I had in my eyes all the tears she had never shed for keeping herself all her life above pity doubt commiseration division, she'd never seen anything to weep over only for Omi would she have wept but in this case being the author of a cowardly action it is herself she would have wept over which would only have aggravated her profound sense of dissatisfaction with herself with the feeling of a further lack of courage: since in her eyes she had not given what she should have given while giving a reason without validity or substance: "It looks like I want to rid myself of a burden" she'd told herself "which however was not a valid argument" she told herself later on, but then it was too late and she hadn't been heroic when she should have been when the time came, which would have been much more charitable than to have let someone without her wits about her suffer go on living for nothing at all. Says my mother course still fixed on the truth. But for George she had only to take the death that Destiny had handed her.

—Ask her—says the book—no I say—ask her if she has forgotten says the book—but it's an absurd question I say—but all the same—I asked: You have forgotten all that. And as I expected she answers: Yes.

I shall go no further I say. I'm even returning over old ground here.

In the big armchairs at my brother's we have stopped struggling pressing one against the others so tightly. I open my hands. One does not take back the child one has given. I must stop I tell myself. I closed the book. I contemplated them. My mother my brother the parents of my son the dead.

My brother weeping my mother not weeping for my son. I let the door to the Clinic fall shut behind me.

Translator's Notes

5
dim nestling
Le niais means "simpleton"; also *nyas* or *eyas,* "an unfledged hawk." A homophone, *le nié,* means "one who is denied."

6
the fault of language
Faute de langue means both "the fault of" and "the lack of."

7
peace: Pay
In French the words *paix* and *paie* are homophones.

7
mussels . . . shells
In French *moules* can mean either "mussels" or "molds."

9
Blue as an angel
The French phrase *le premier bleu jour de l'ange,* from *le jour de l'an* (New Year's Day), plays on the similarity in sound of *an* (year) and *ange* (angel).

11
the fault of . . . the fault of
In French *faute, faute de, il faut, défaut* can mean "fault," "the fault of," "flaw," "defect," "to need," and "for lack of." See note, page 6.

13
divide myself
Partager can mean "to divide" or "to share."

15
out of sight
French *à pied de vue* is a play on two expressions: *à pied de* (at the foot of) and *à perte de vue* (as far as one can see). It has overtones of both distance and loss (*perte*).

16
in every sense
French *dans tous les sens* means "in all directions" but also suggests "in every sense of the word" and "in every sense" (of the five senses).

17
lily of the valley
In France, on the First of May (*la Fête du Travail,* Labor Day), it is customary to offer lilies of the valley, sold in the streets in sprigs or pots.

19
I surrender
French *je me rends* means "I go" or, depending on context, "I surrender." Here both meanings come into play.

20
plateau
French *plateau:* "plateau" and "tray."

26
eternal flame tarnished by oil
The French *éternie* is a neologism which combines *éternel* and *terni* (tarnished) into a single word.

27
for lack of thought and the fault of words
French *faute de.* See notes for pages 6 and 11.

28
undone, fended off and defended and de-fended
In French *fendre* means "to split" but sounds like *fondre,* "to melt," and has the same root as *défendre,* "to defend" or "to de-fend."

28
She can't get over it
Elle n'en revient pas: "she can't get over it," but also, literally, "she does not come back."

28
what has happened
Ce qui vient d'arriver: "what has just happened," but also, literally, "what has just arrived."

28
who doesn't look like
Qui n'a pas l'air: "who doesn't look like," but also, literally, "who hasn't got air."

29
What has happened . . . has not arrived
See note, page 28.

31
A Nose Newborn
In French *un nouveau nez* means "a new nose" but also suggests its homophone, *un nouveau né,* "a newborn."

35
in person . . . no-one-in-person
En personne: "in person," but also "no one."

35
my unconscious loss, my loss of consciousness
Ma perte de connaissance: "my loss of consciousness," but also, literally, "my loss of knowledge."

36
less crude
Moins cru (Latin *crudus,* bleeding) means "less raw/crude," but also "less believed in" (*croire* from Latin *credere,* to believe).

39
less than . . . no longer dogs
French *plus:* "no longer," but also "more" (dog).

39
secondhand
Une question de point de vue et d'occasion can also mean "a matter of occasion."

61
Gnawing at me
Me remordent: "bite again," "remorse."

83
niche
French *niche:* "nest" as well as "niche."

89
recemetery
The French word is *récimetière,* a neologism made by joining *récit* (tale) to *cimetière* (cemetery).

About the Author

Hélène Cixous is a French writer, philosopher, playwright, critic, and activist who continues to influence writers, scholars, and feminists around the world. Her recent works include *Reveries of the Wild Woman* and *The Third Body,* both published by Northwestern University Press, and *Veils* (with Jacques Derrida), *Portrait of Jacques Derrida as a Young Jewish Saint, The Writing Notebooks,* and *Dream I Tell You.*

Avant-Garde & Modernism Collection

General Editor
Rainer Rumold

Avant-Garde & Modernism Studies

General Editors
Marjorie Perloff
Rainer Rumold